Black Woman Coloring Book For Teens

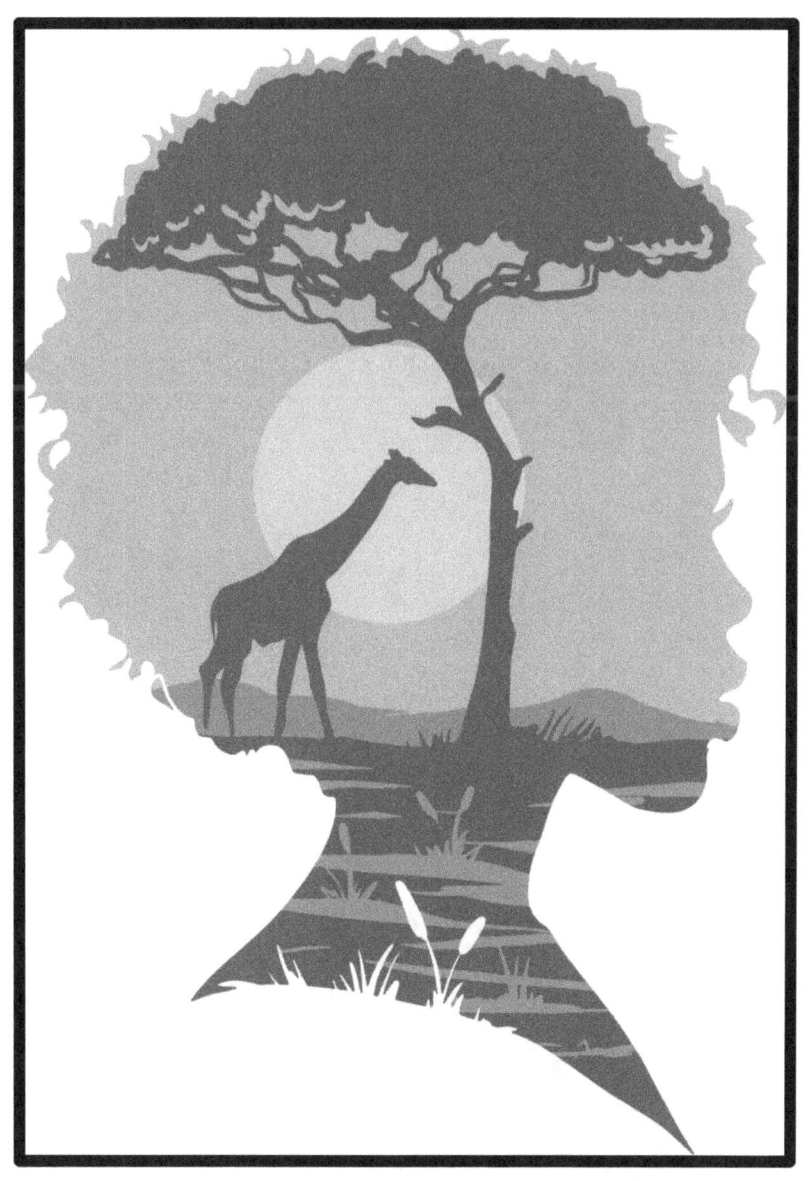

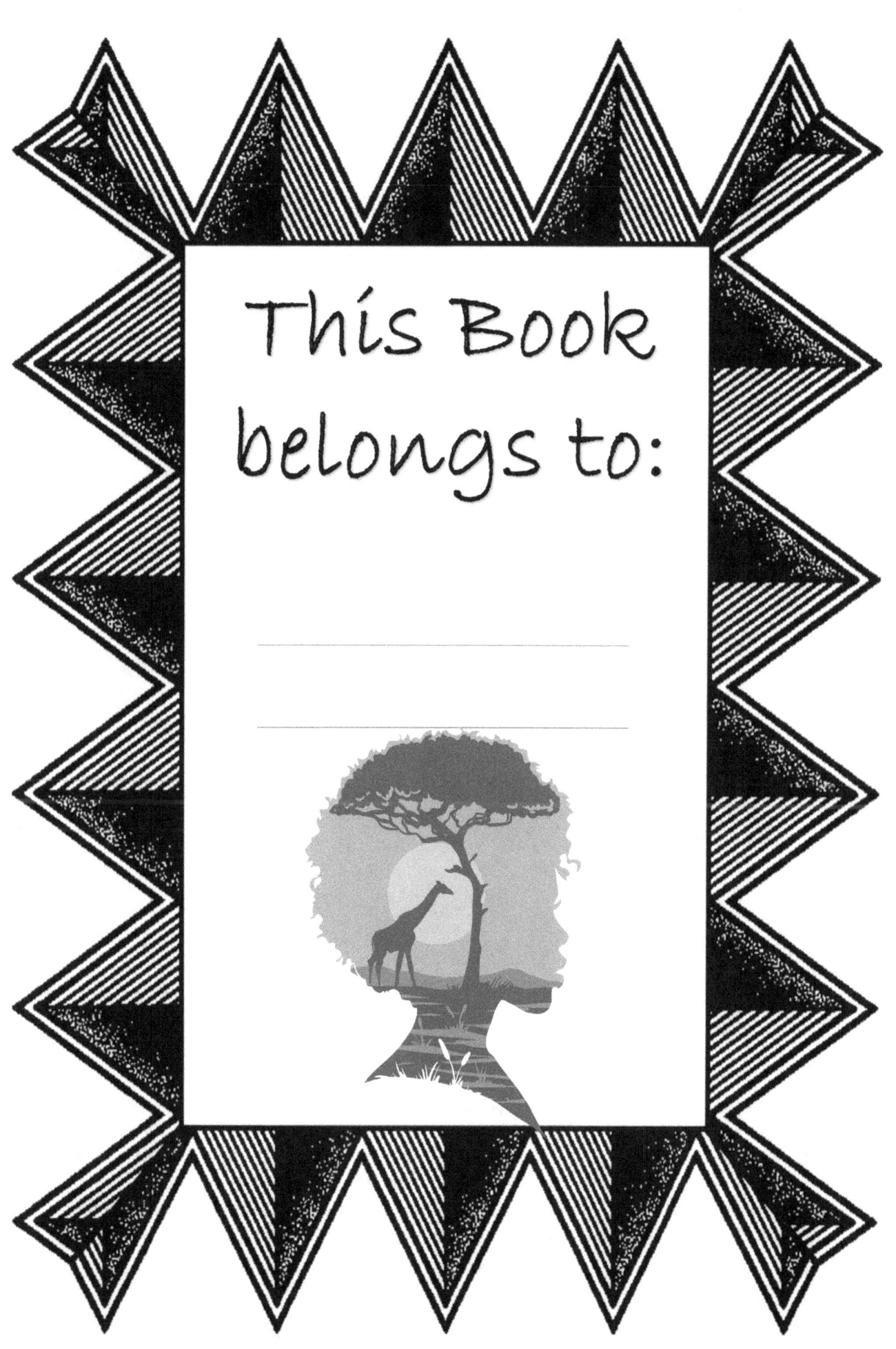

This Book
belongs to:

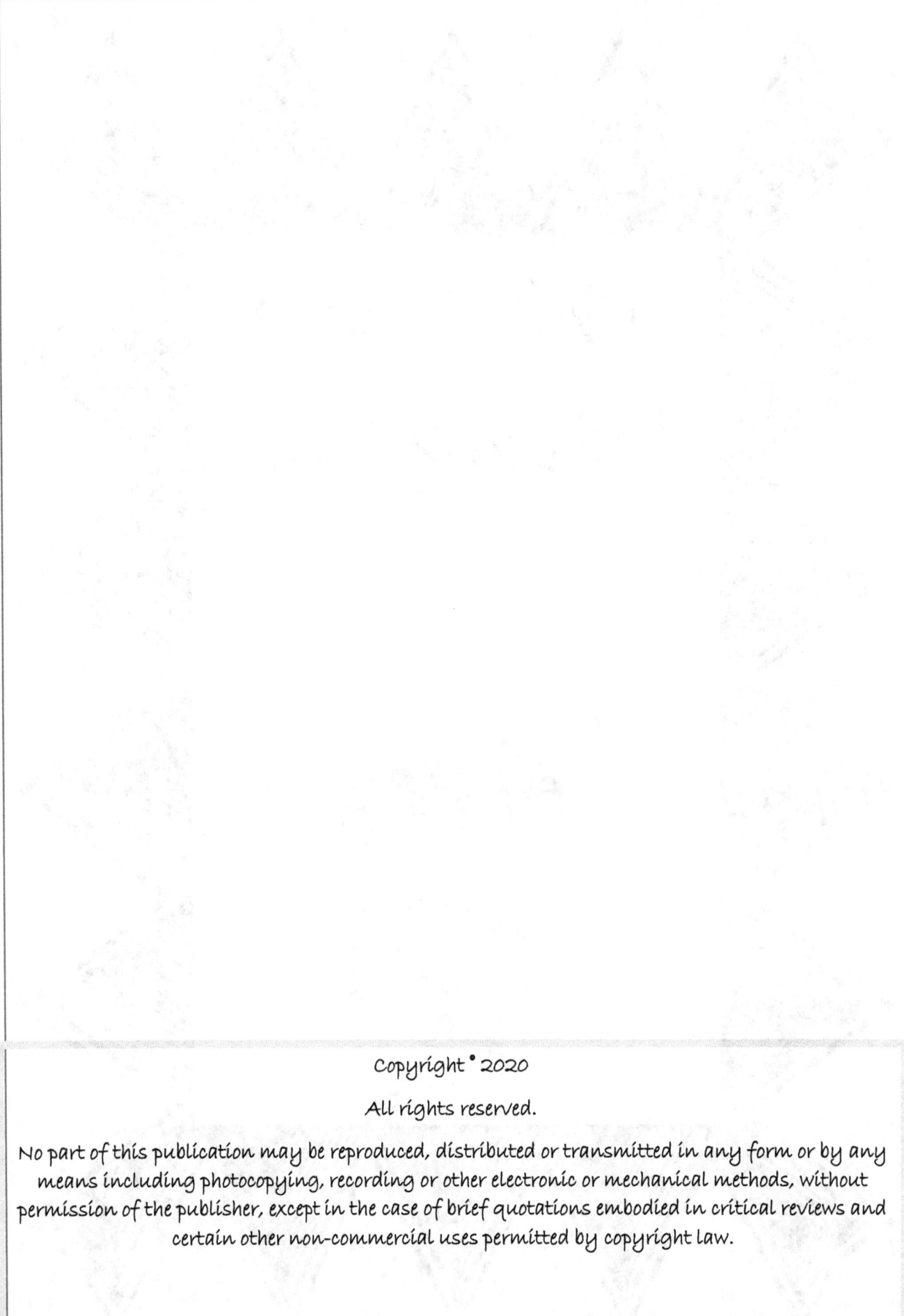

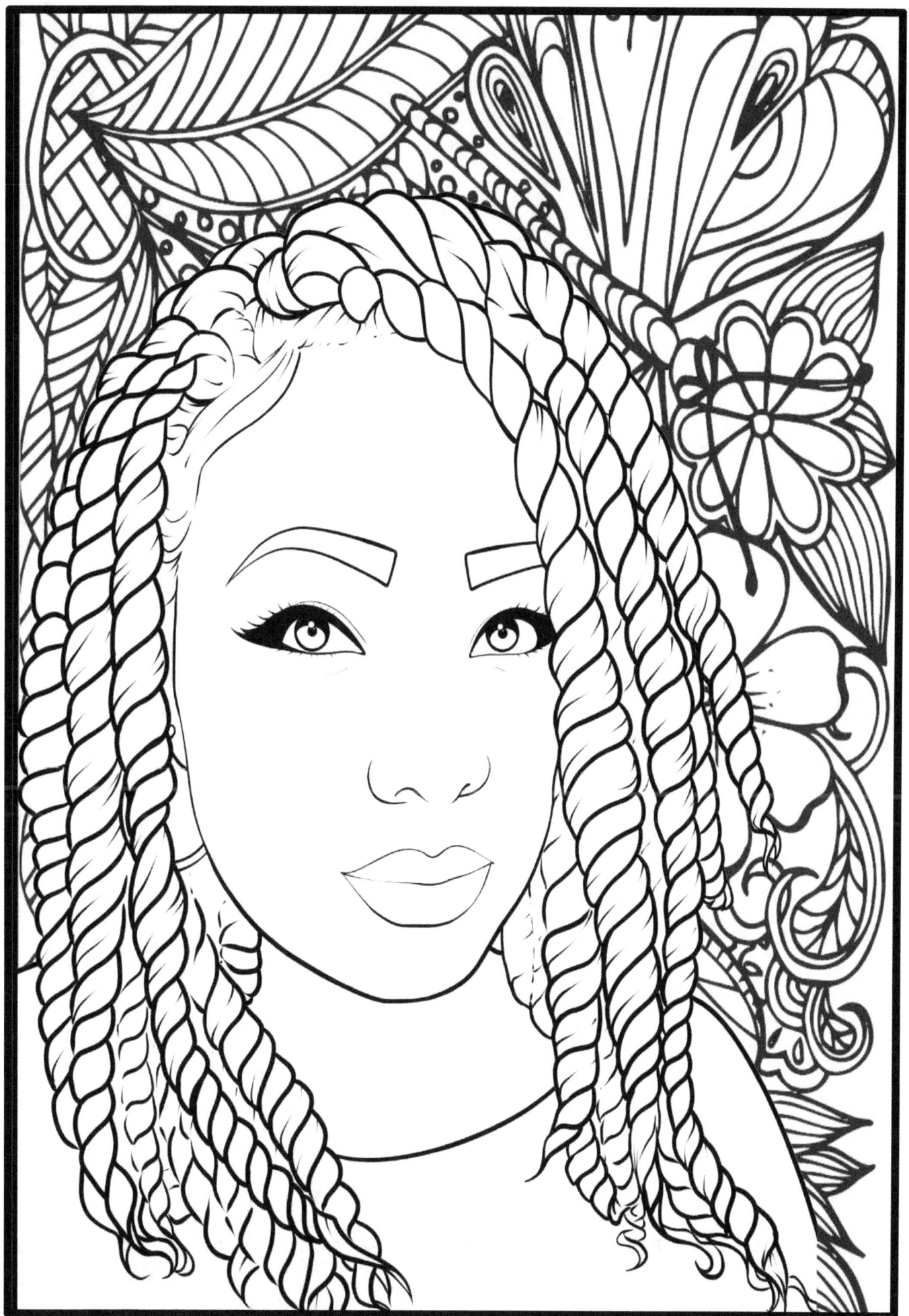

Passion is energy. Feel the power that comes from focusing on what excites you.

- Oprah Winfrey

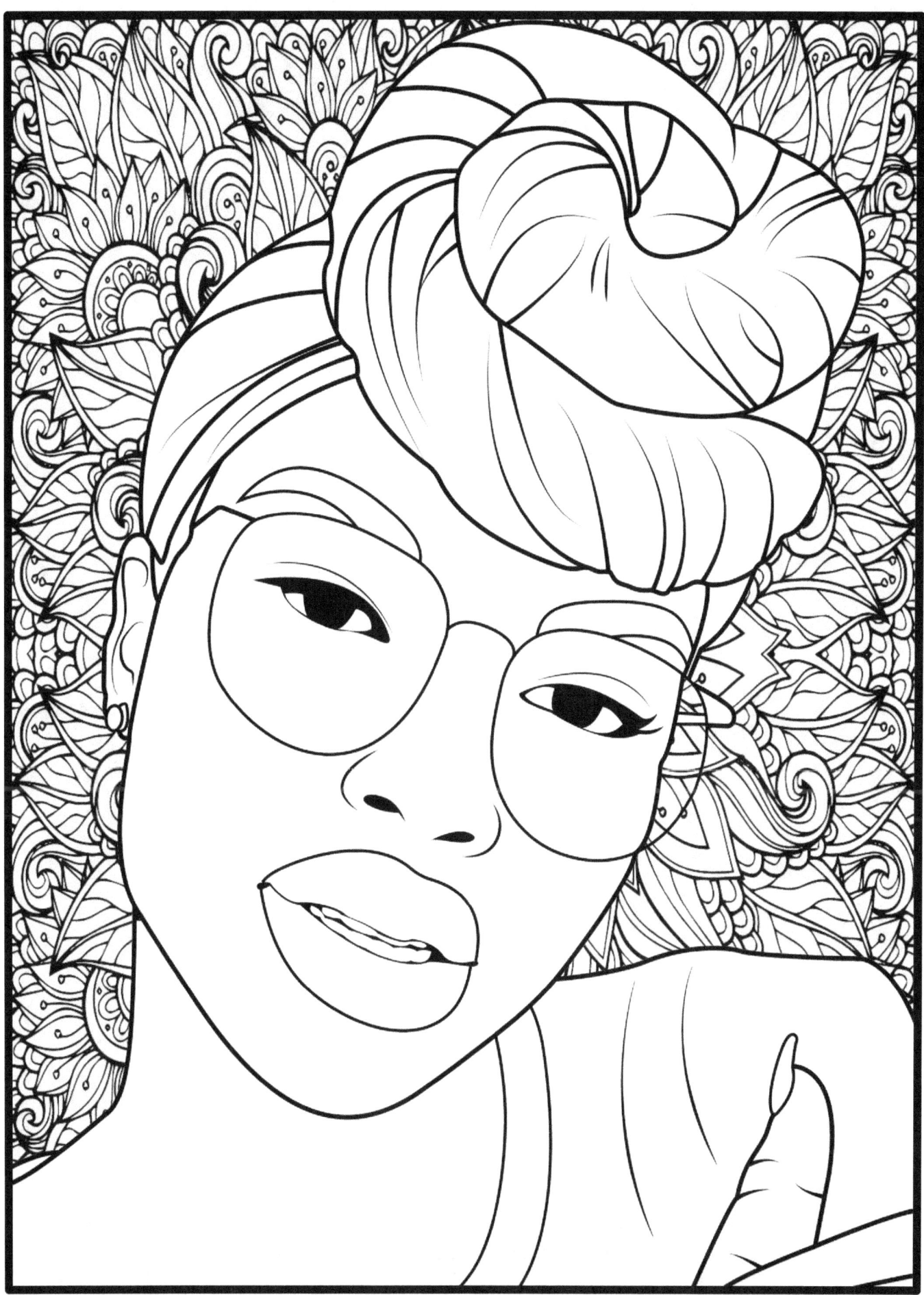

My philosophy is that not only are you responsible for your life, but doing the best at this moment puts you in the best place for the next moment.

- Oprah Winfrey

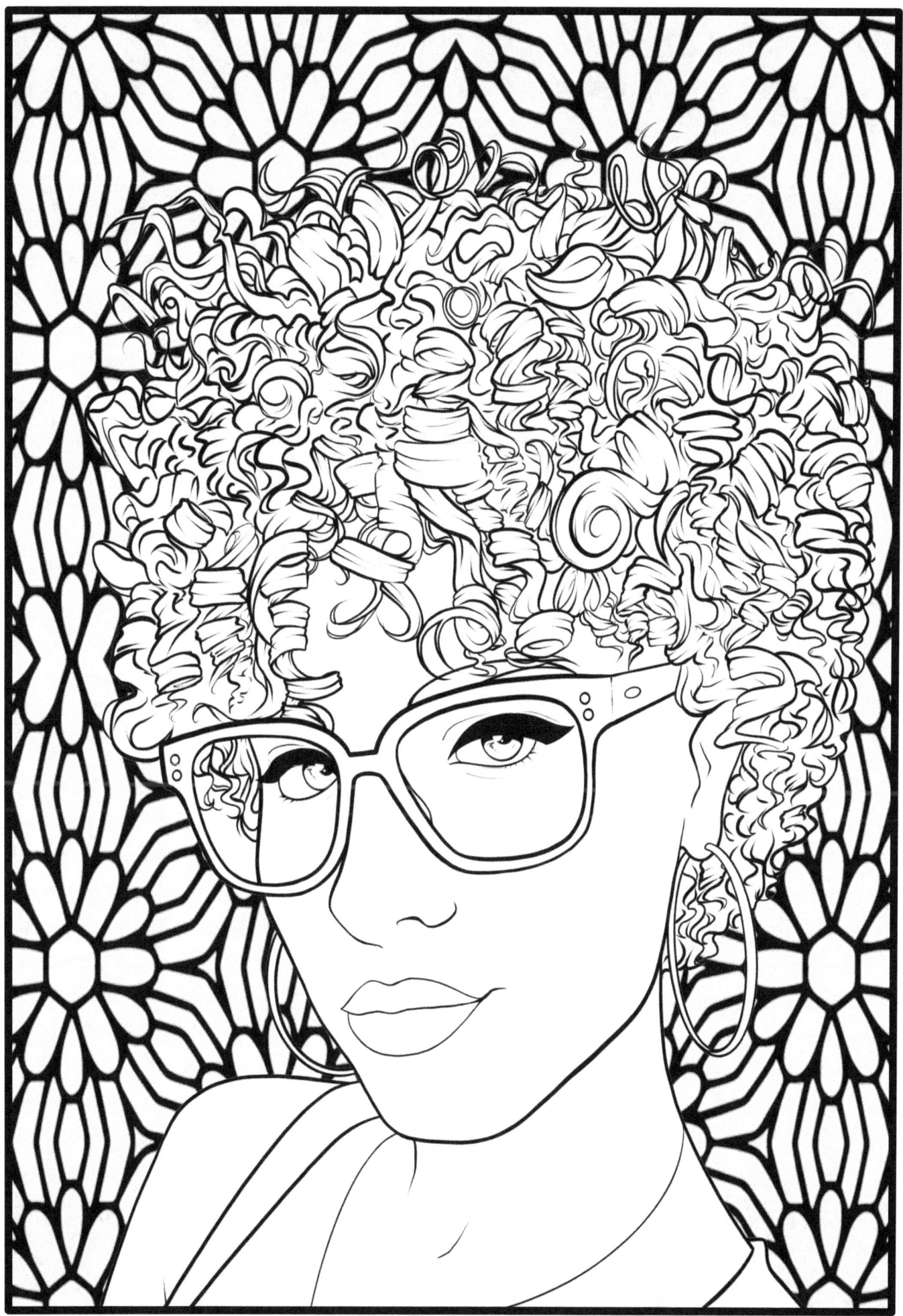

If you are always trying to be normal, you will never know how amazing you can be.

-    Dr. Maya Angelou

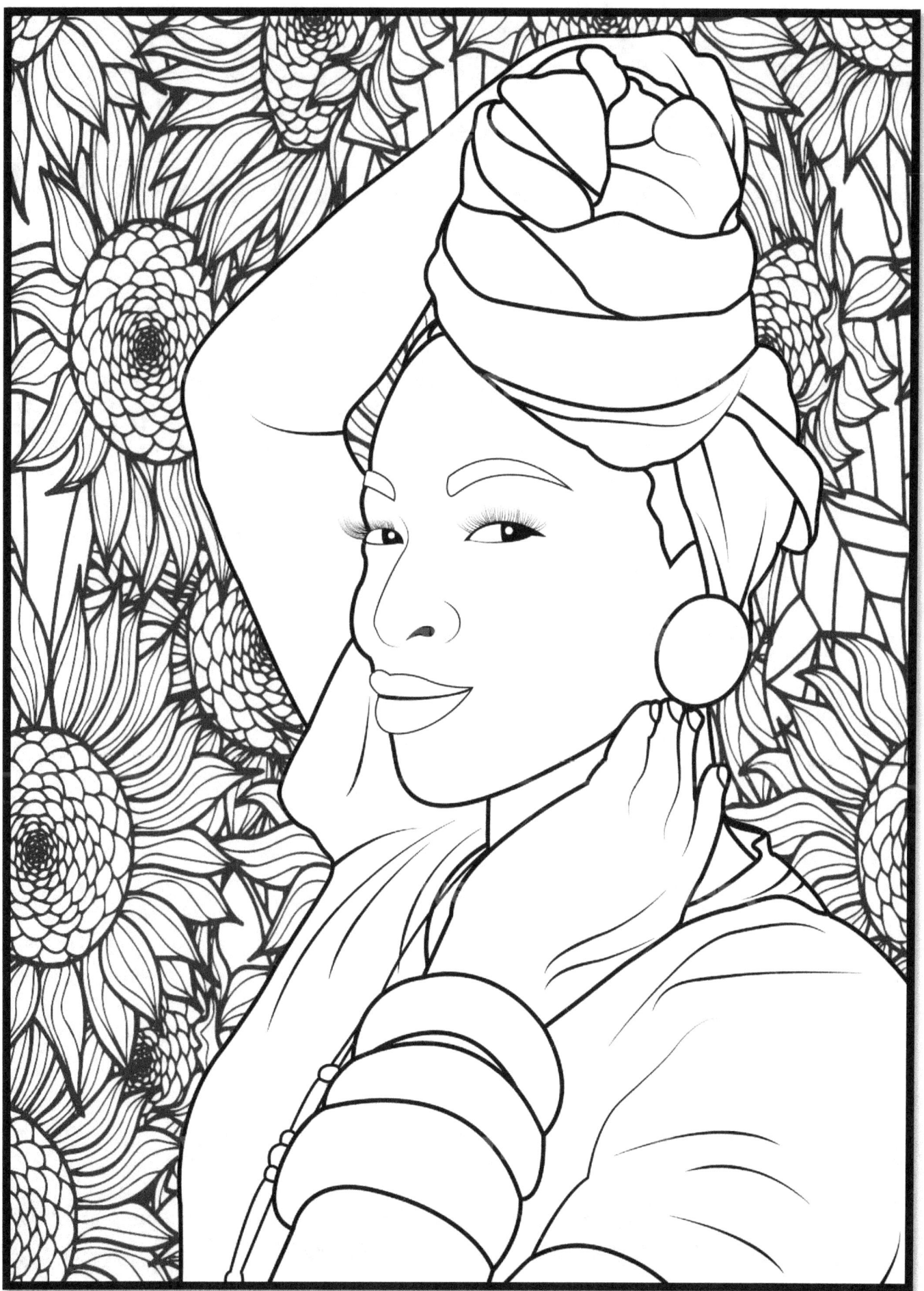

Don't settle for average. Bring your best to the moment. Then, whether it fails or succeeds, at least you know you gave all you had. We need to live the best that's in us.

- Angela Bassett

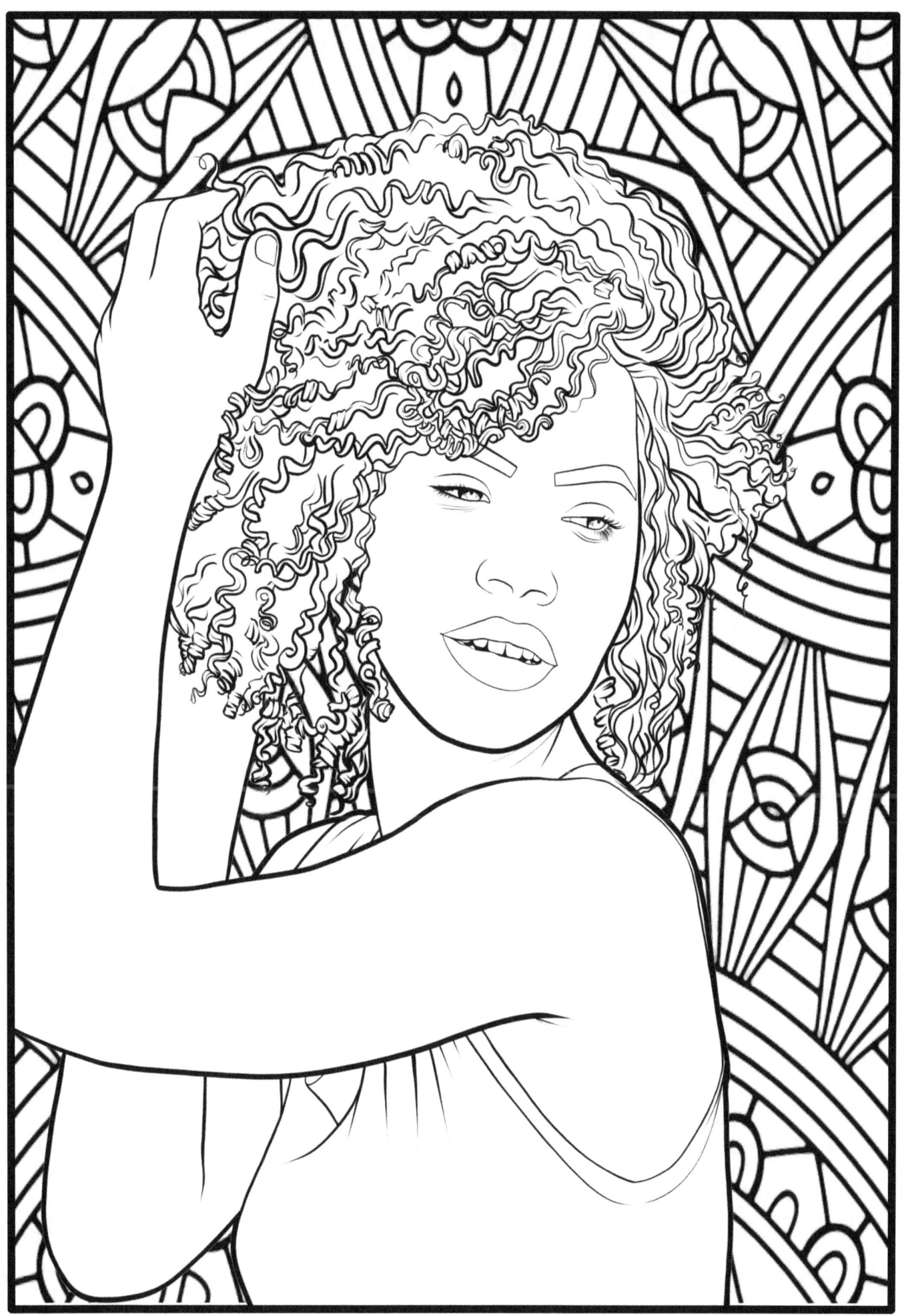

It is so liberating to really know what I want, what truly makes me happy, what I will not tolerate.
I have learned that it is no one else's job to take care of me but me.

- Beyonce Knowles

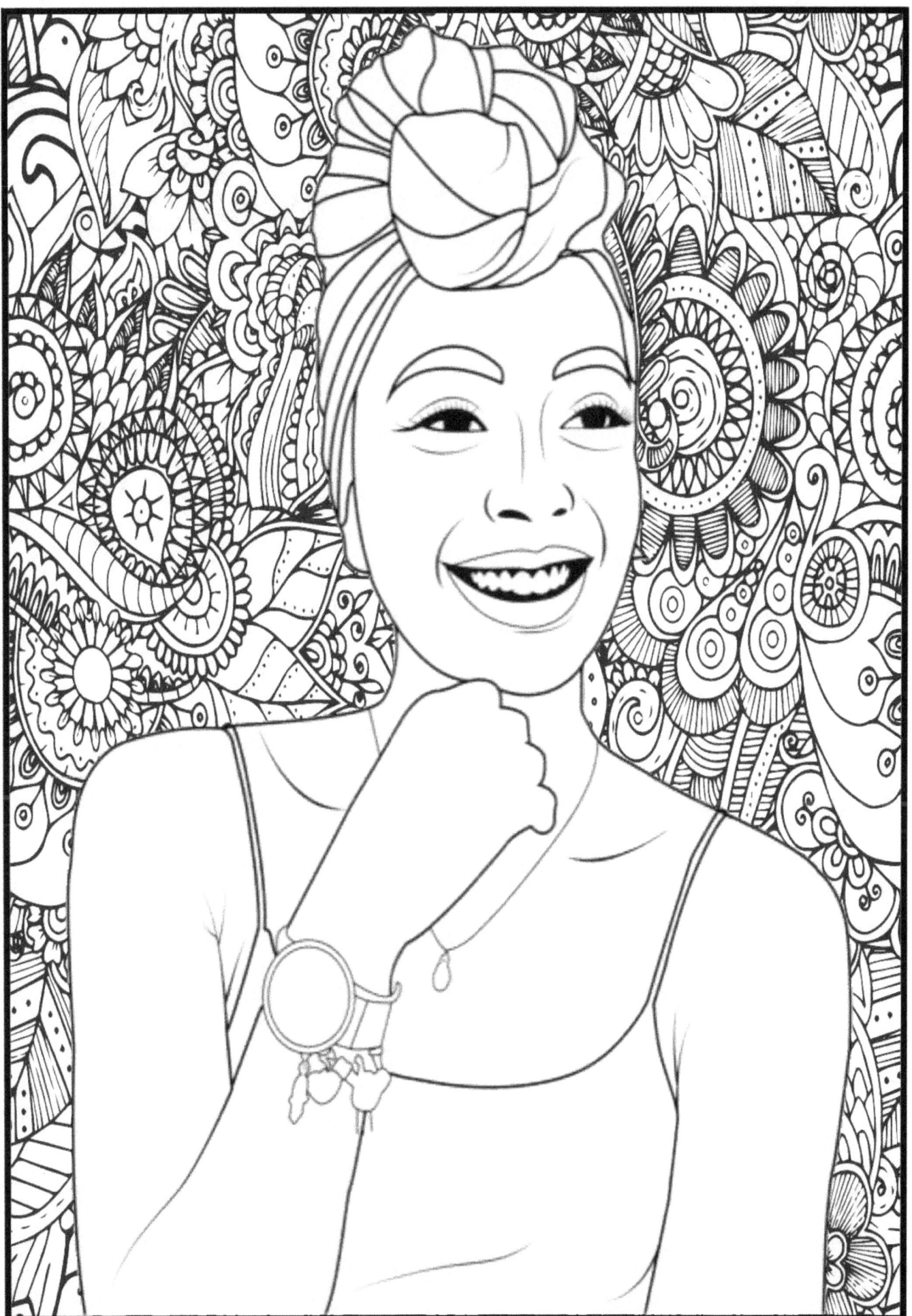

I have standards I don't plan on lowering for anybody ... including myself.

- Zendaya

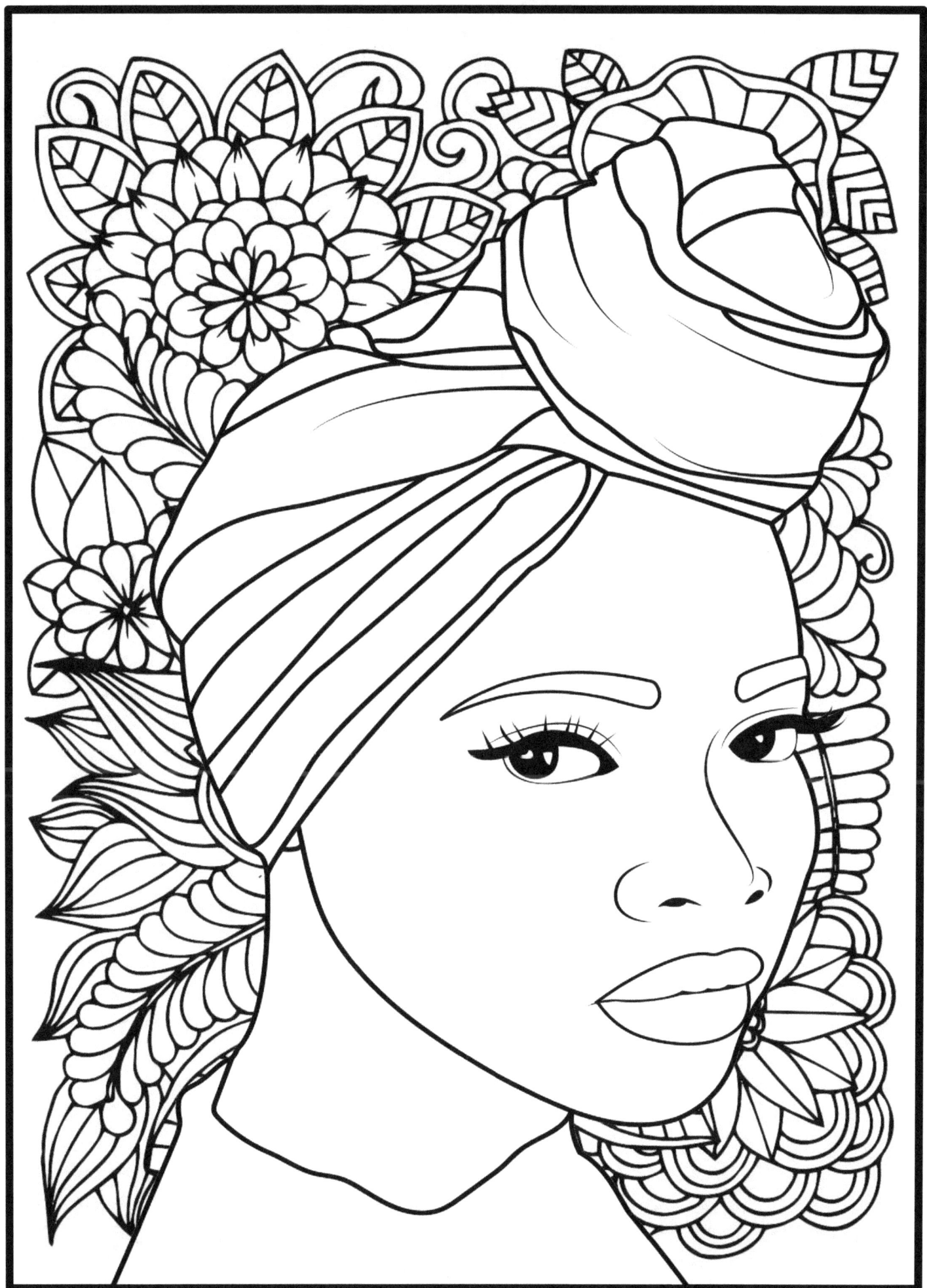

Be proud of who you are, not ashamed of how someone else sees you.

- Unknown

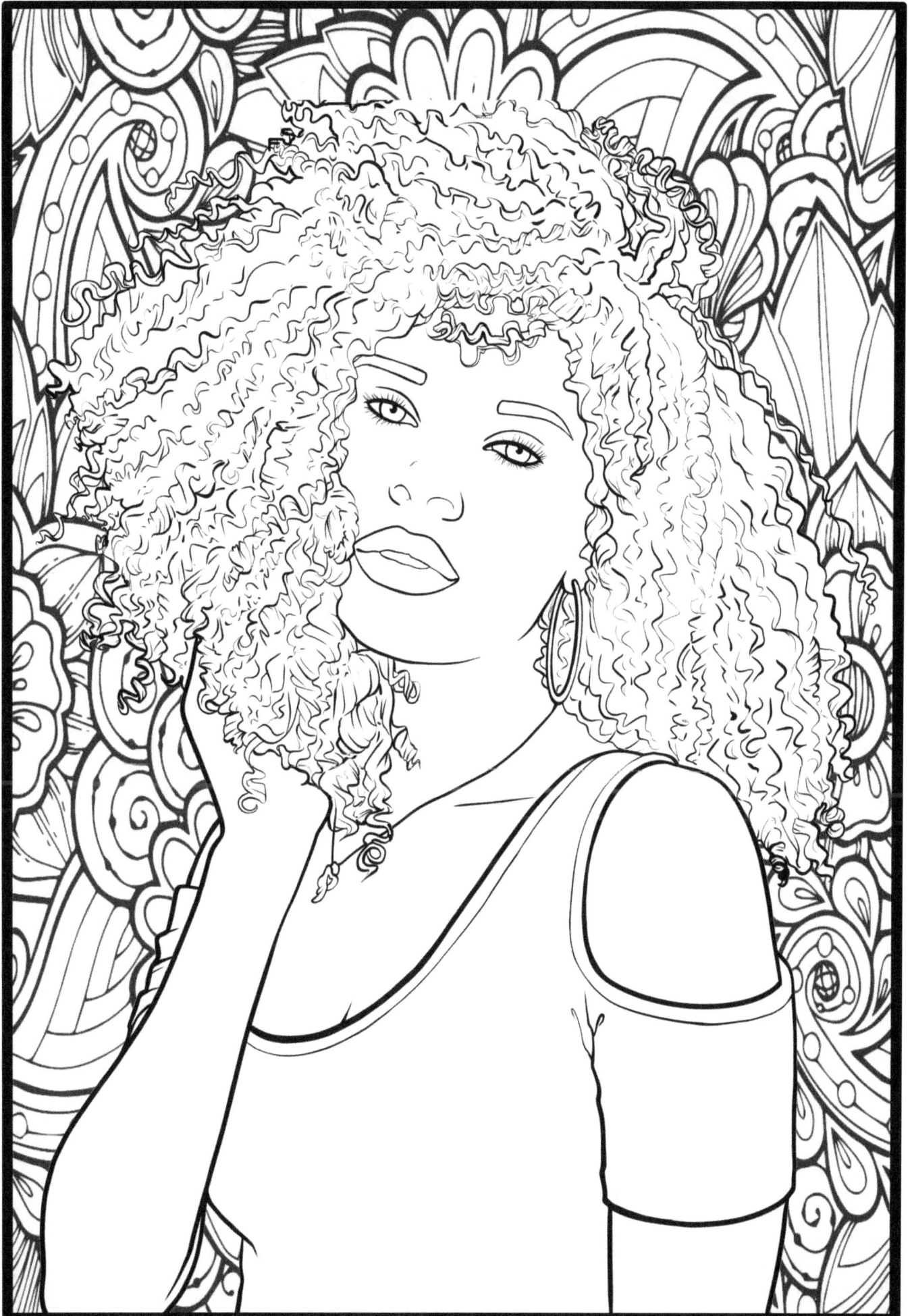

The moment you learn to love yourself, you won't want to be anyone else.
- Rihanna

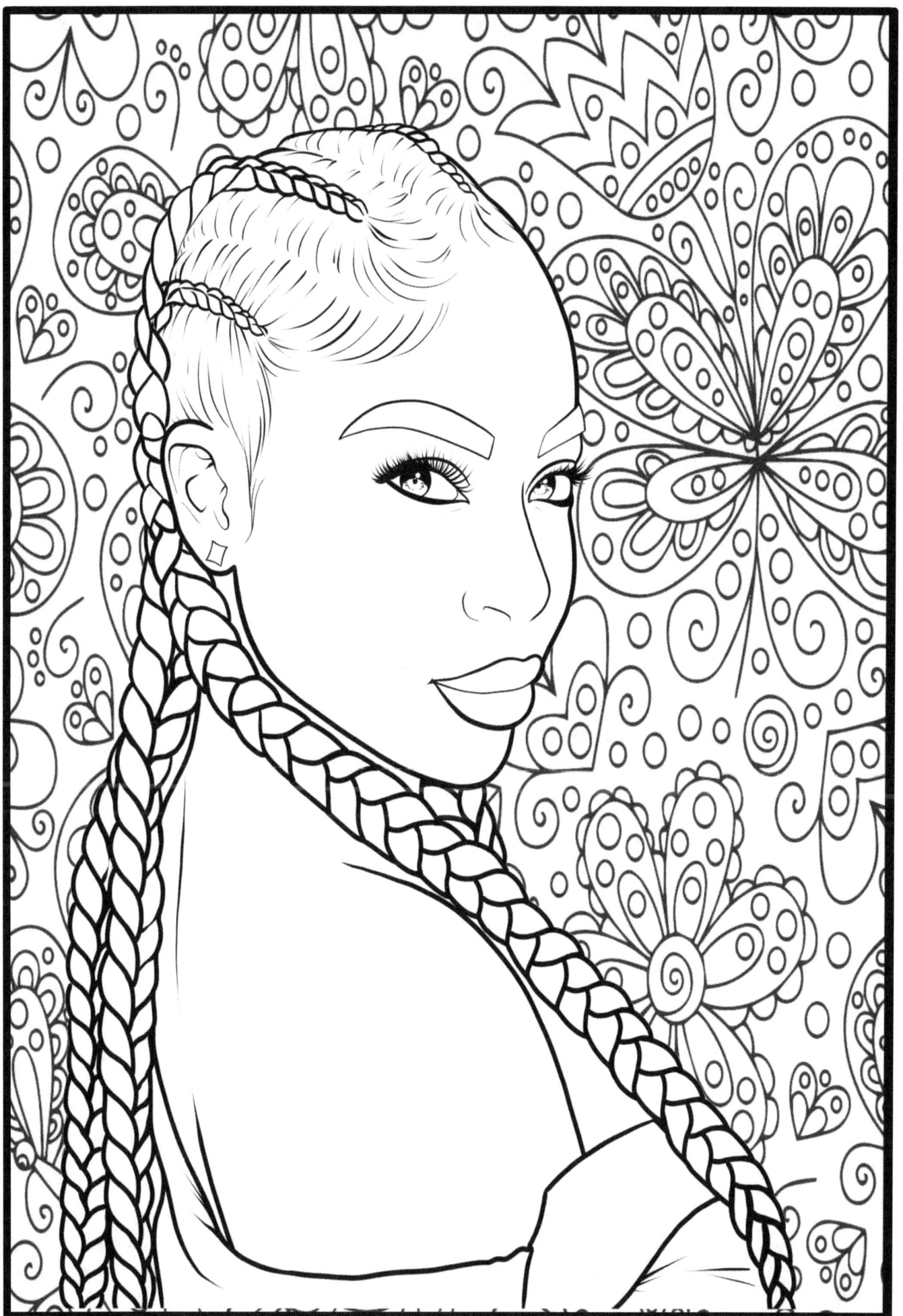

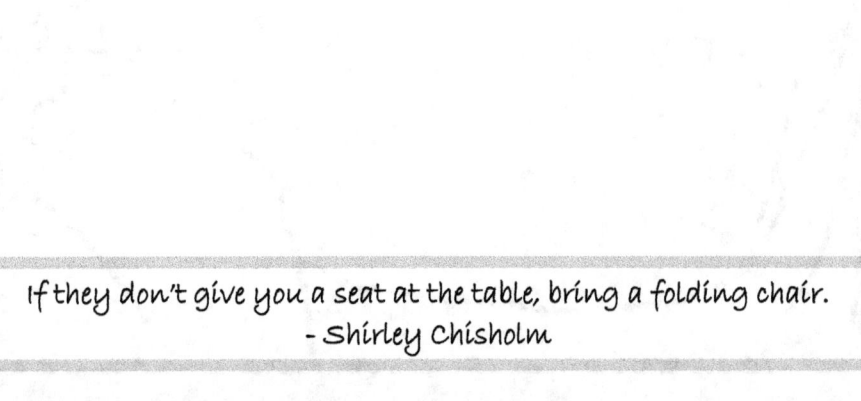
If they don't give you a seat at the table, bring a folding chair.
- Shirley Chisholm

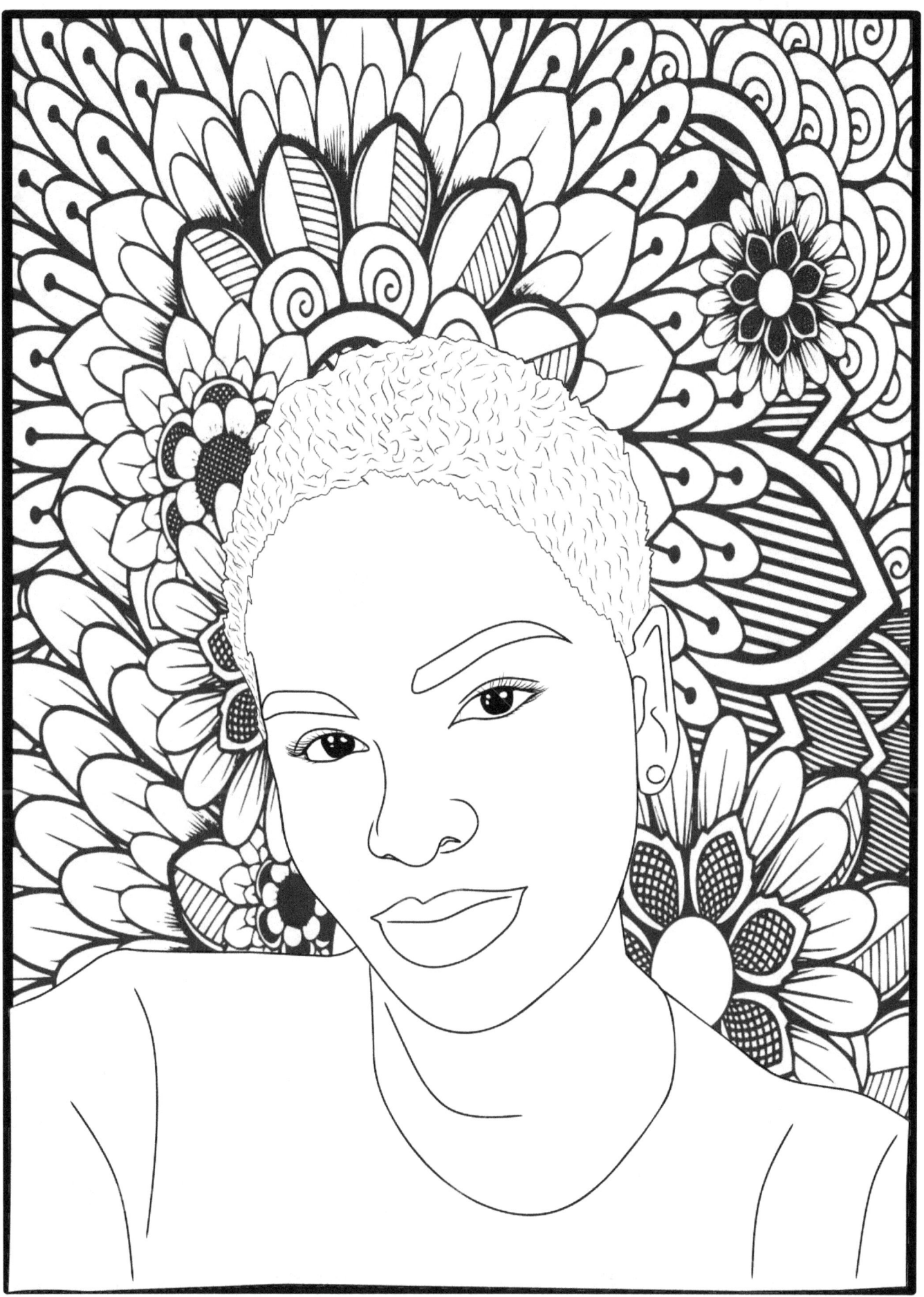

Stand for something or you will fall for anything.
- Rosa Parks

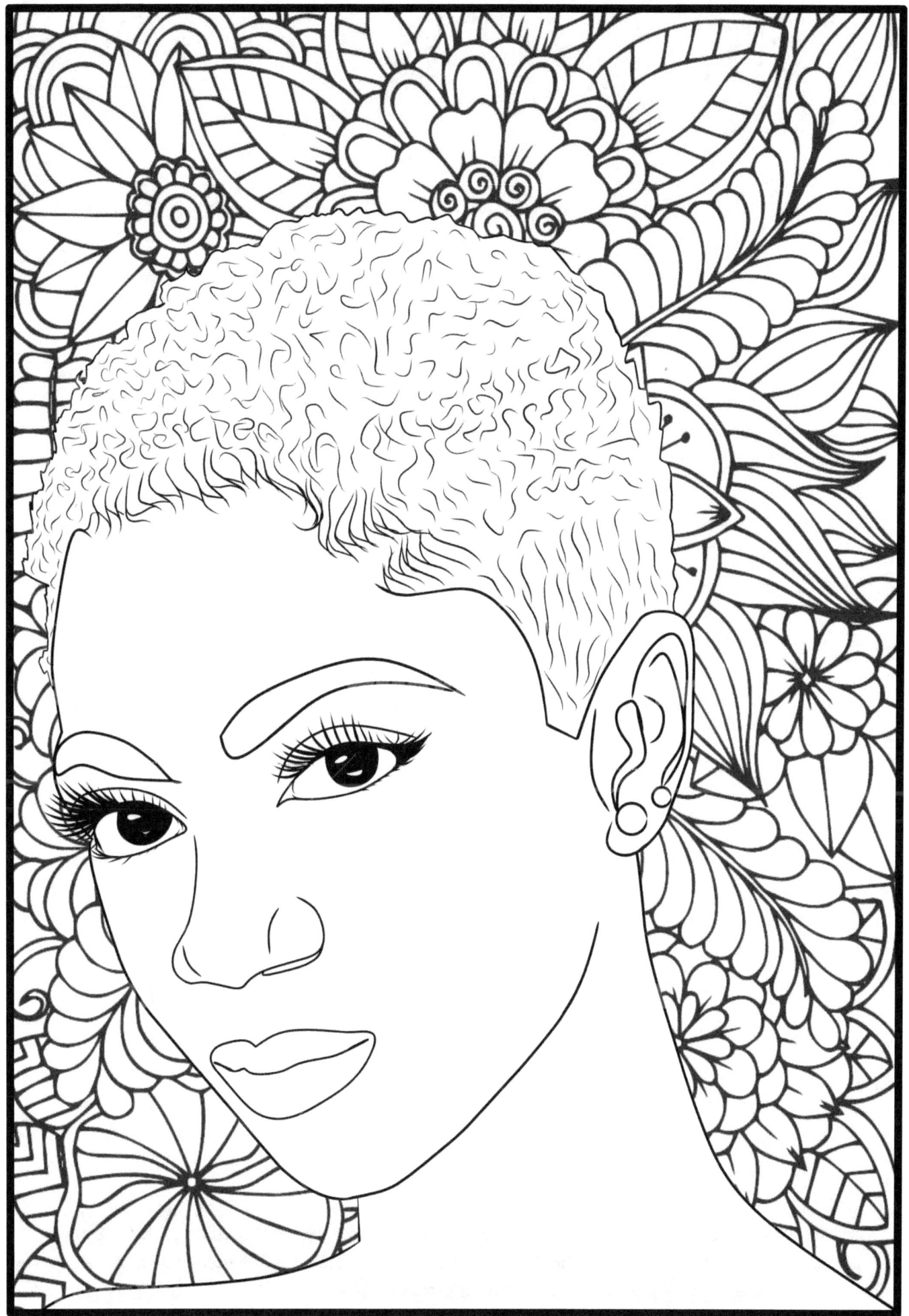

Embrace what makes you unique, even if it makes others uncomfortable. I didn't have to become perfect because I've learned throughout my journey that perfection is the enemy of greatness.
- Janelle Monae

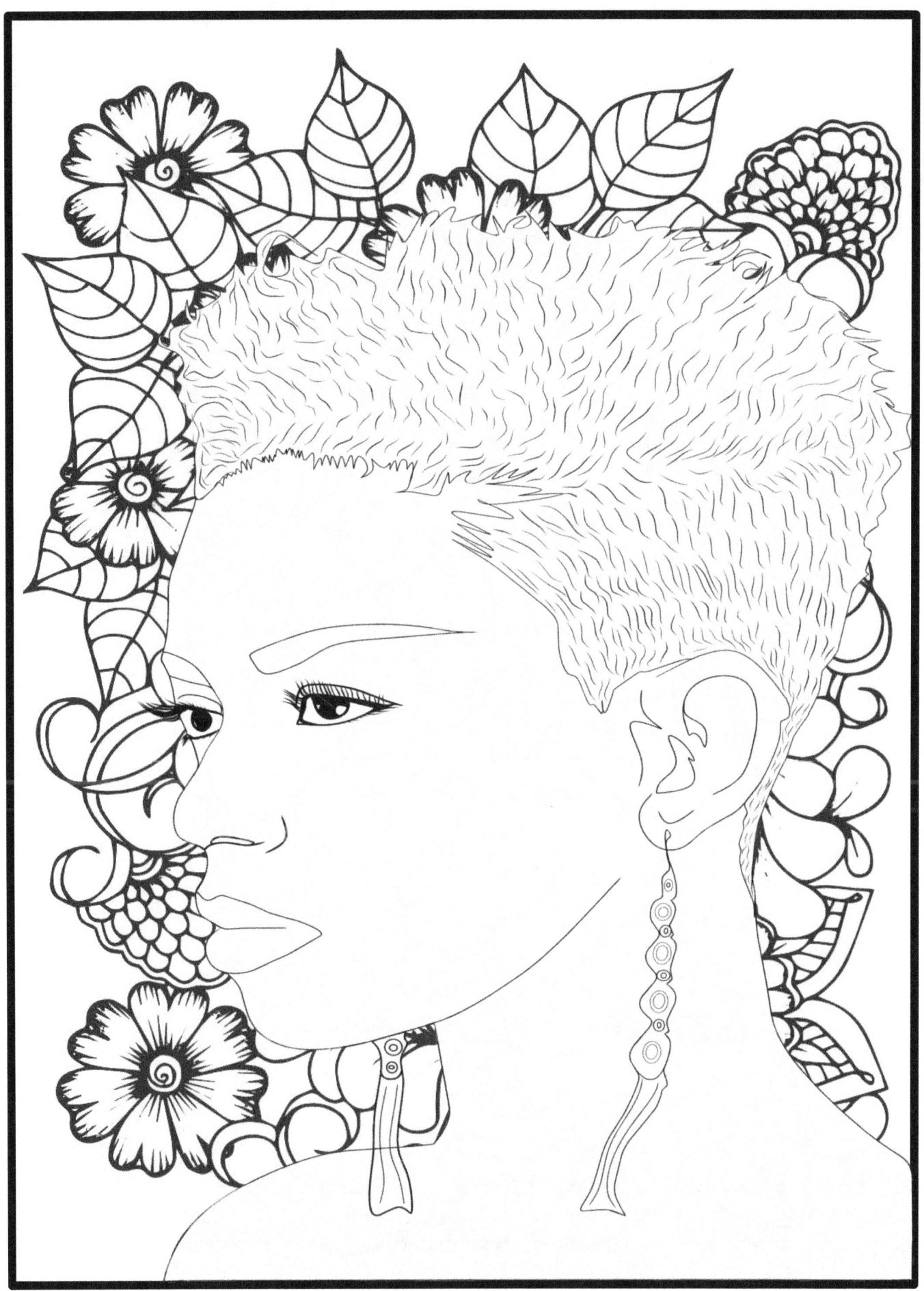

You may not always have a comfortable life and you will not always be able to solve all of the world's problems at once but don't ever underestimate the importance you can have because history has shown us that courage can be contagious and hope can take on a life of its own.

- Michelle Obama

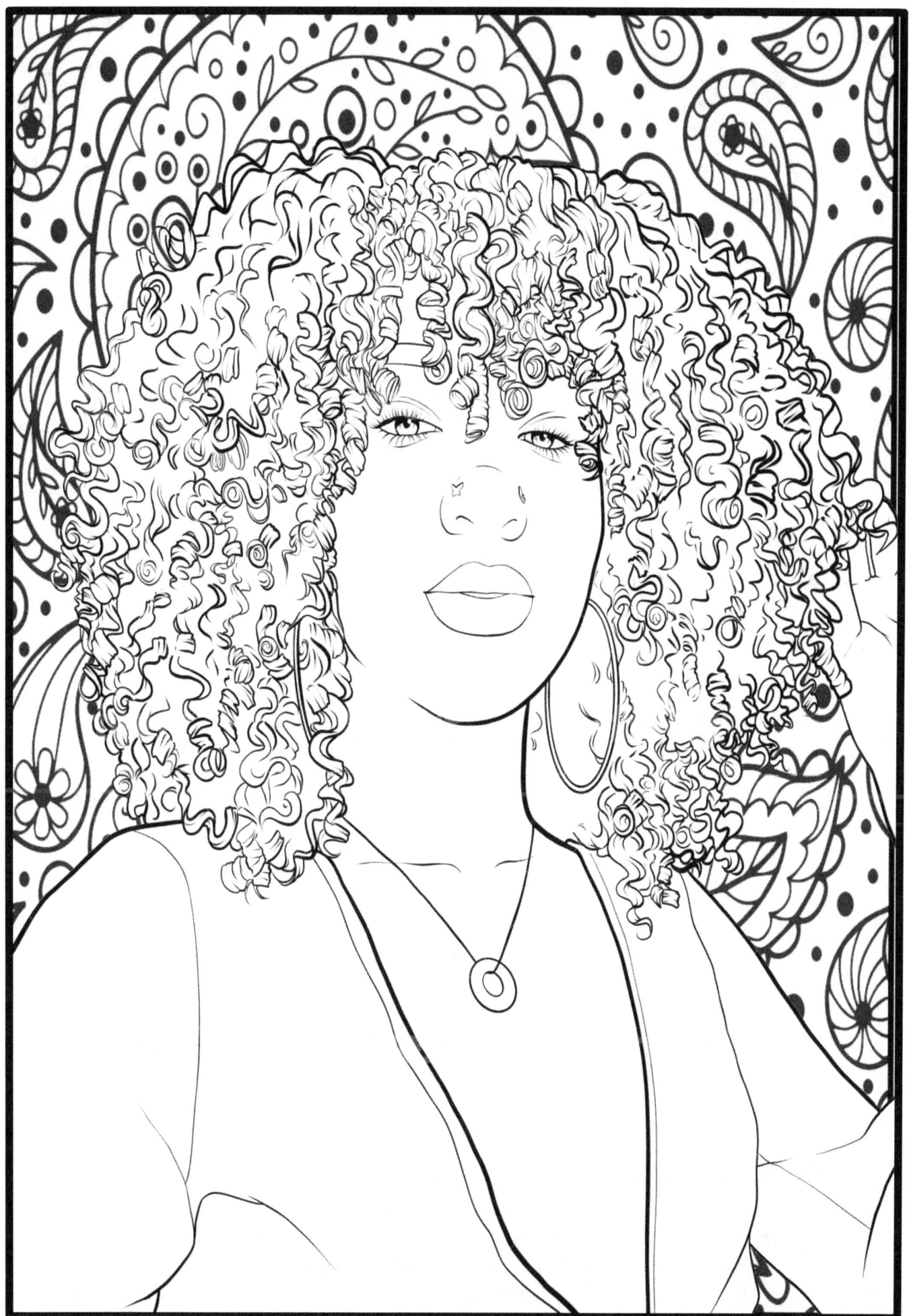

Girls of all kinds can be beautiful -- from the thin, plus-sized, short, very tall, ebony to porcelain-skinned; the quirky, clumsy, shy, outgoing, and all in between. It's not easy though because many people still put beauty into a confining, narrow box ... Think outside of the box ... Pledge that you will look in the mirror and find the unique beauty in you.
- Tyra Banks

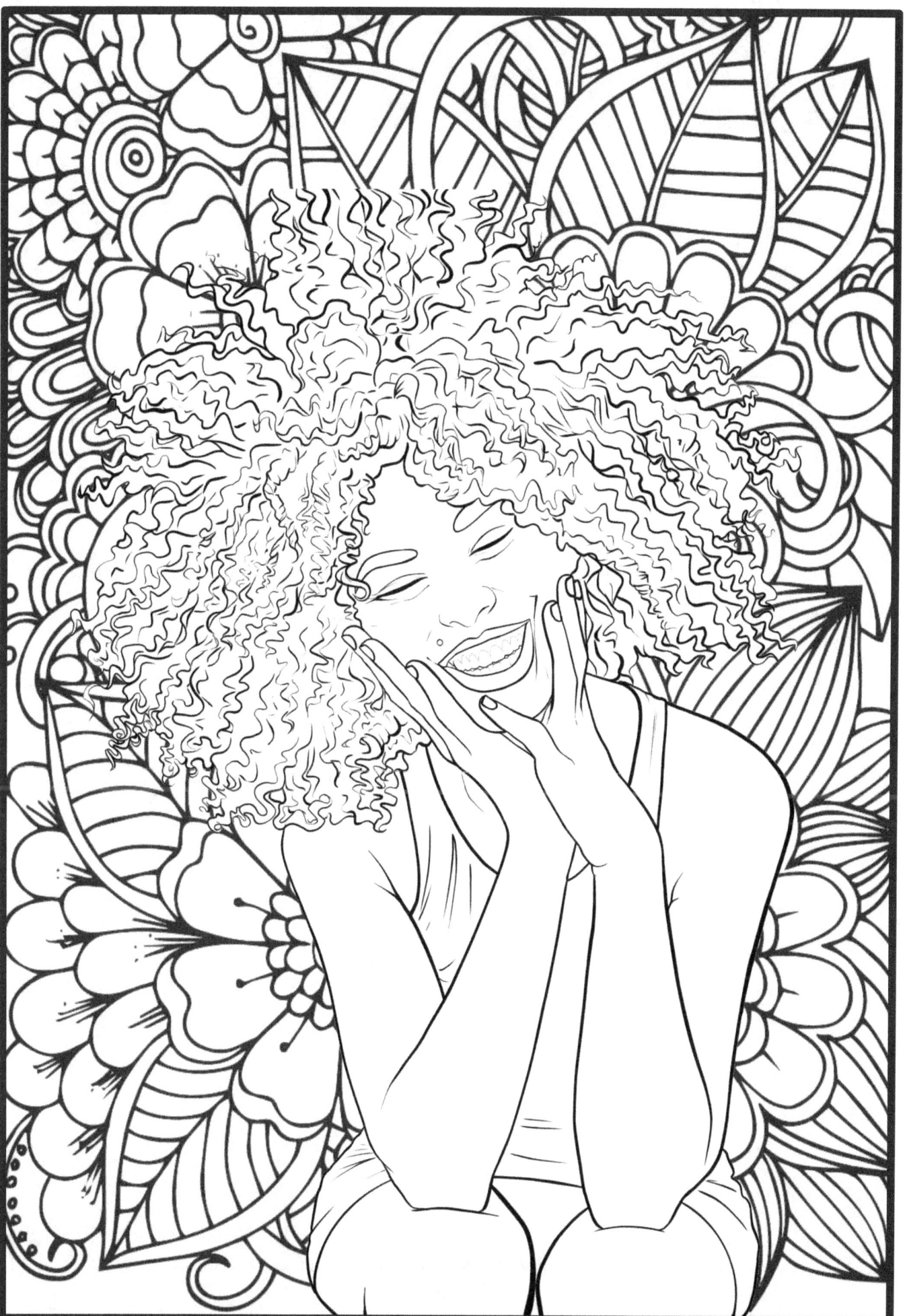

I'd rather regret the risks that didn't work out than the chances I didn't take at all.
- Simone Biles

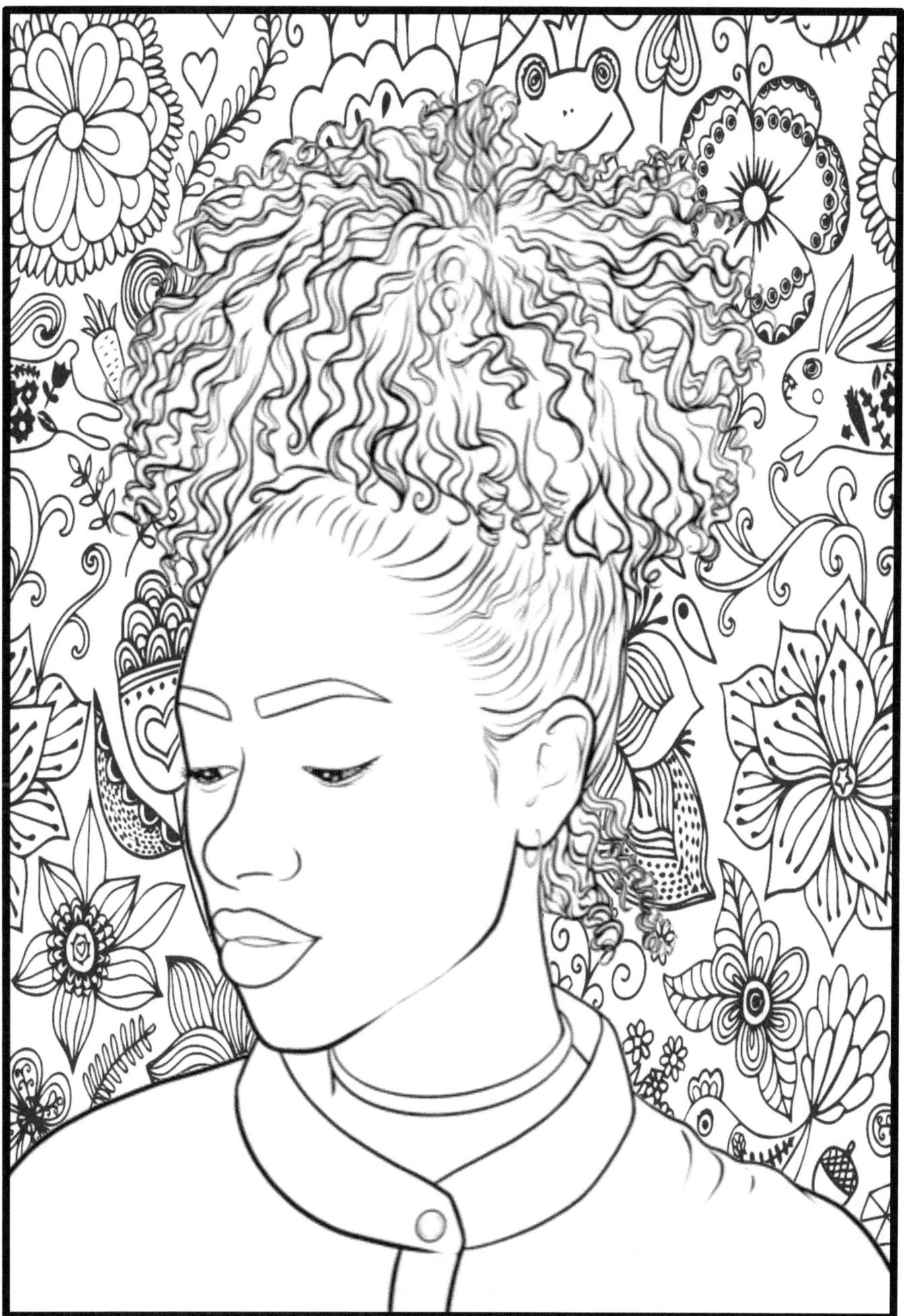

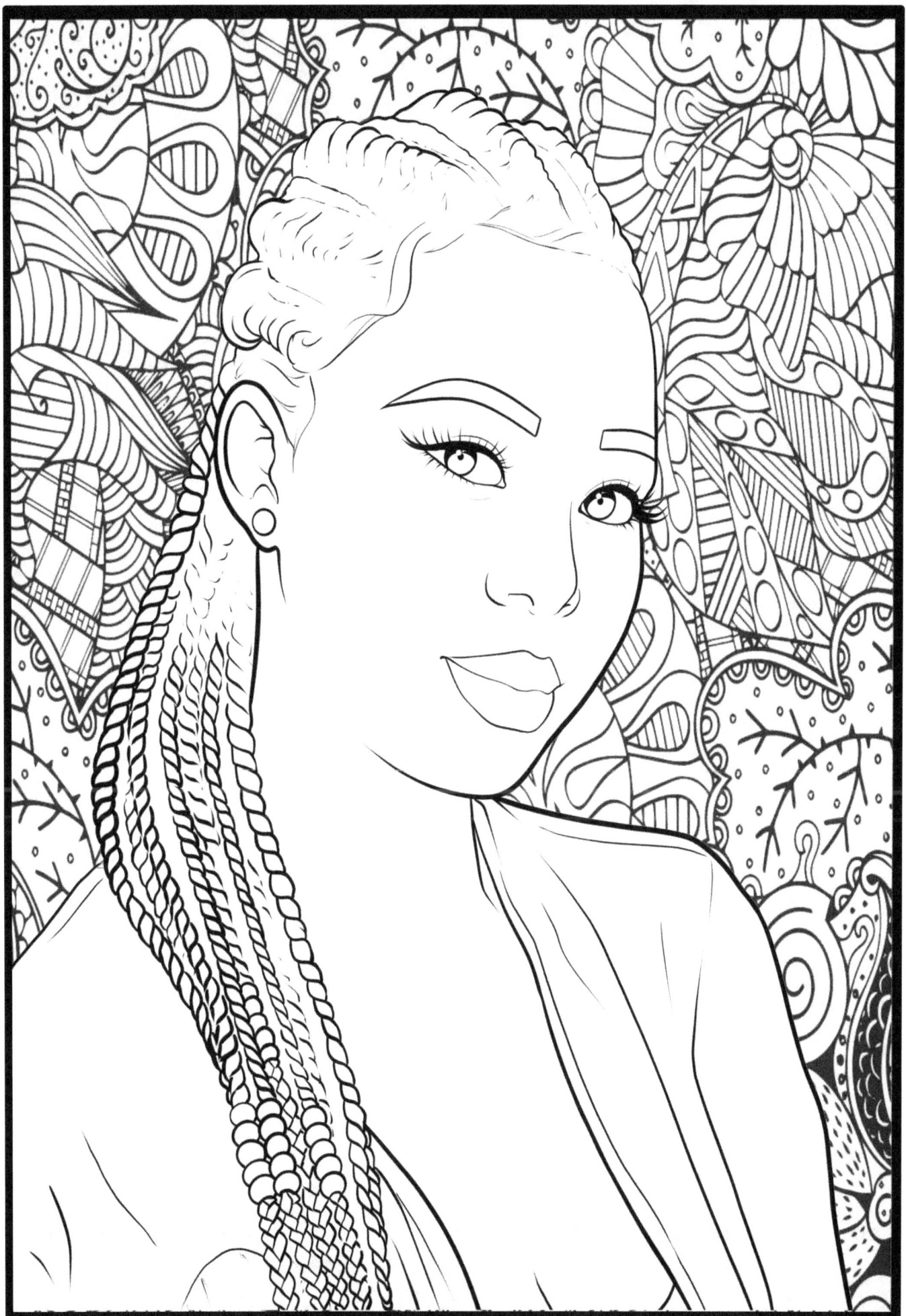

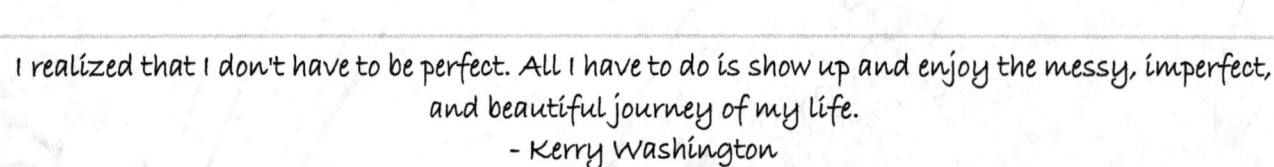
I realized that I don't have to be perfect. All I have to do is show up and enjoy the messy, imperfect, and beautiful journey of my life.
- Kerry Washington

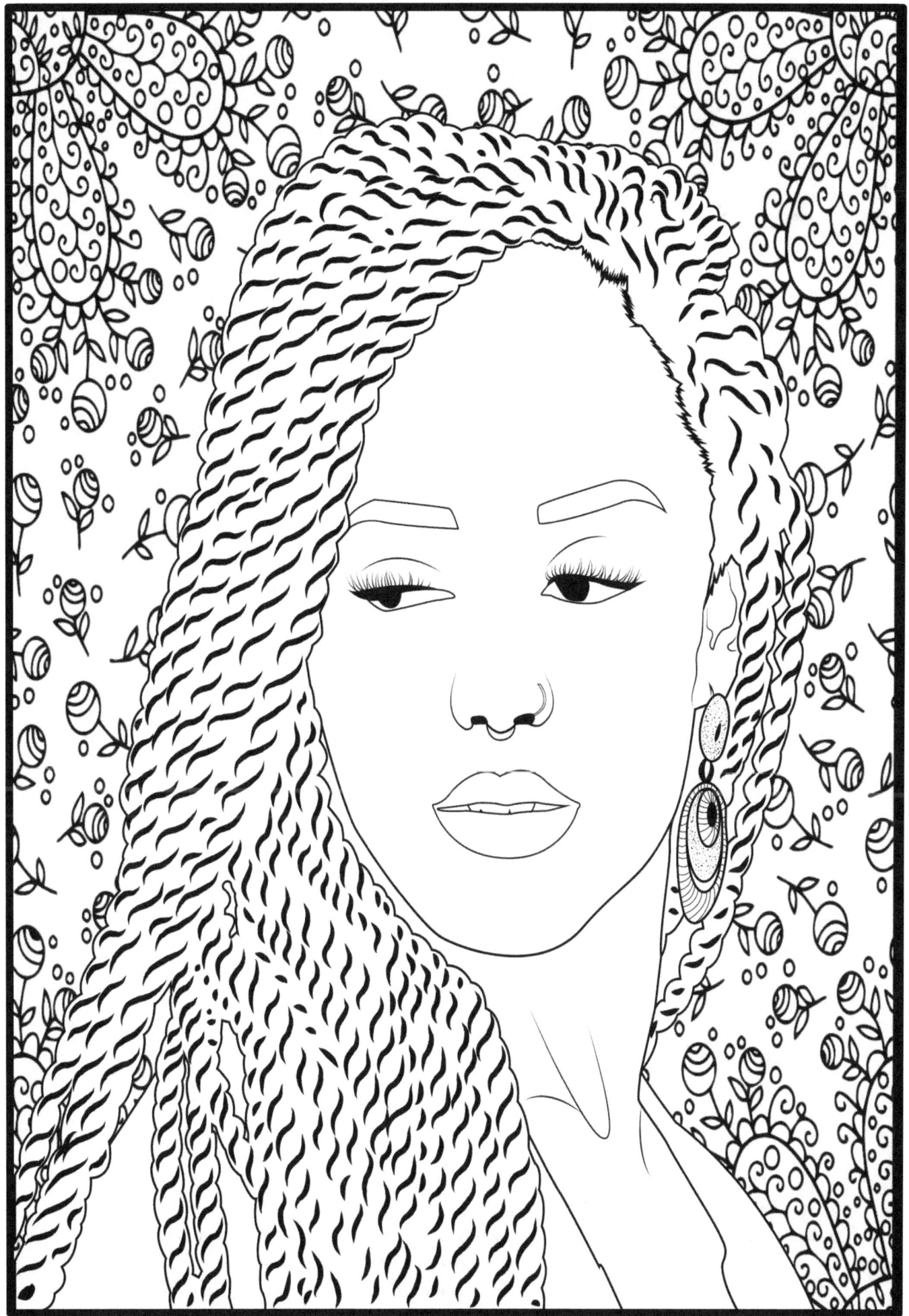

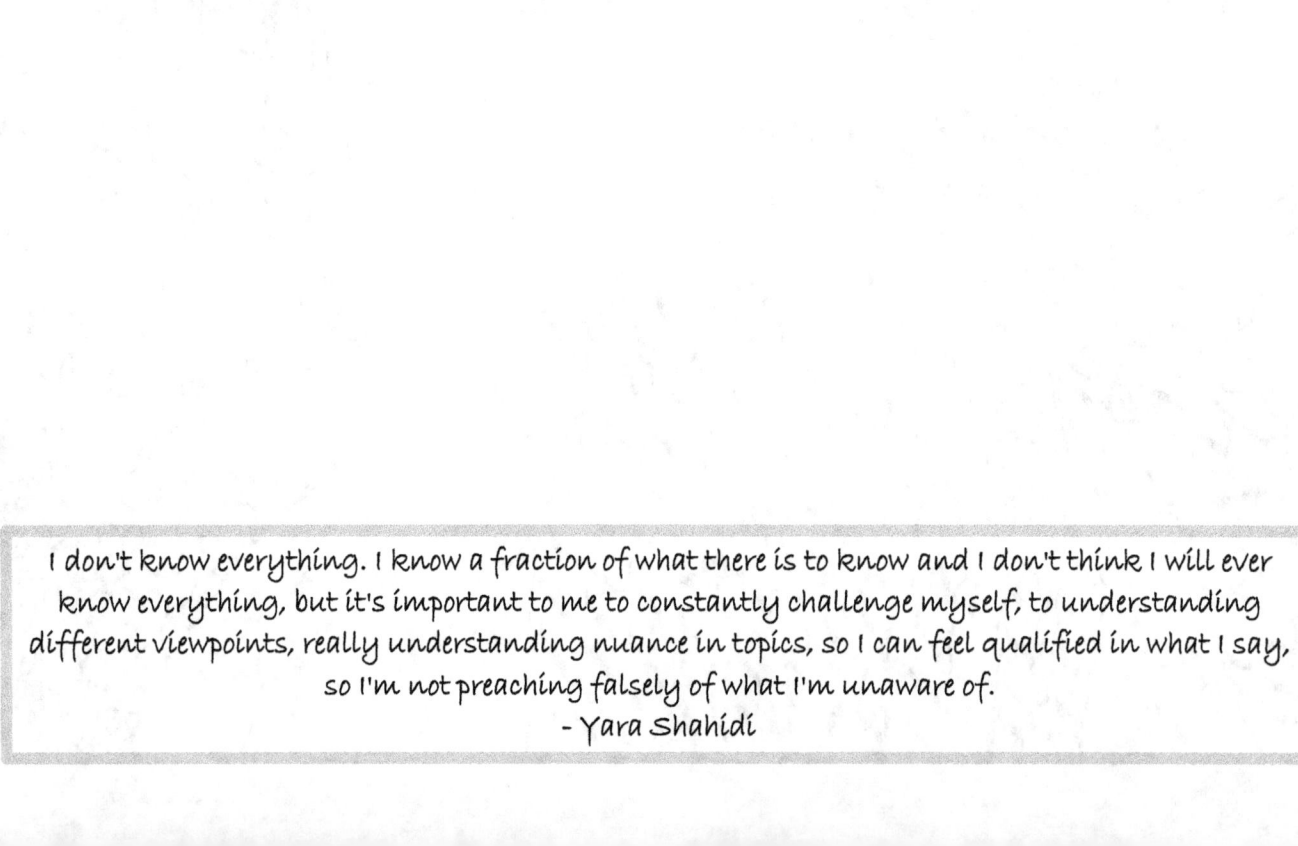
I don't know everything. I know a fraction of what there is to know and I don't think I will ever know everything, but it's important to me to constantly challenge myself, to understanding different viewpoints, really understanding nuance in topics, so I can feel qualified in what I say, so I'm not preaching falsely of what I'm unaware of.
- Yara Shahidi

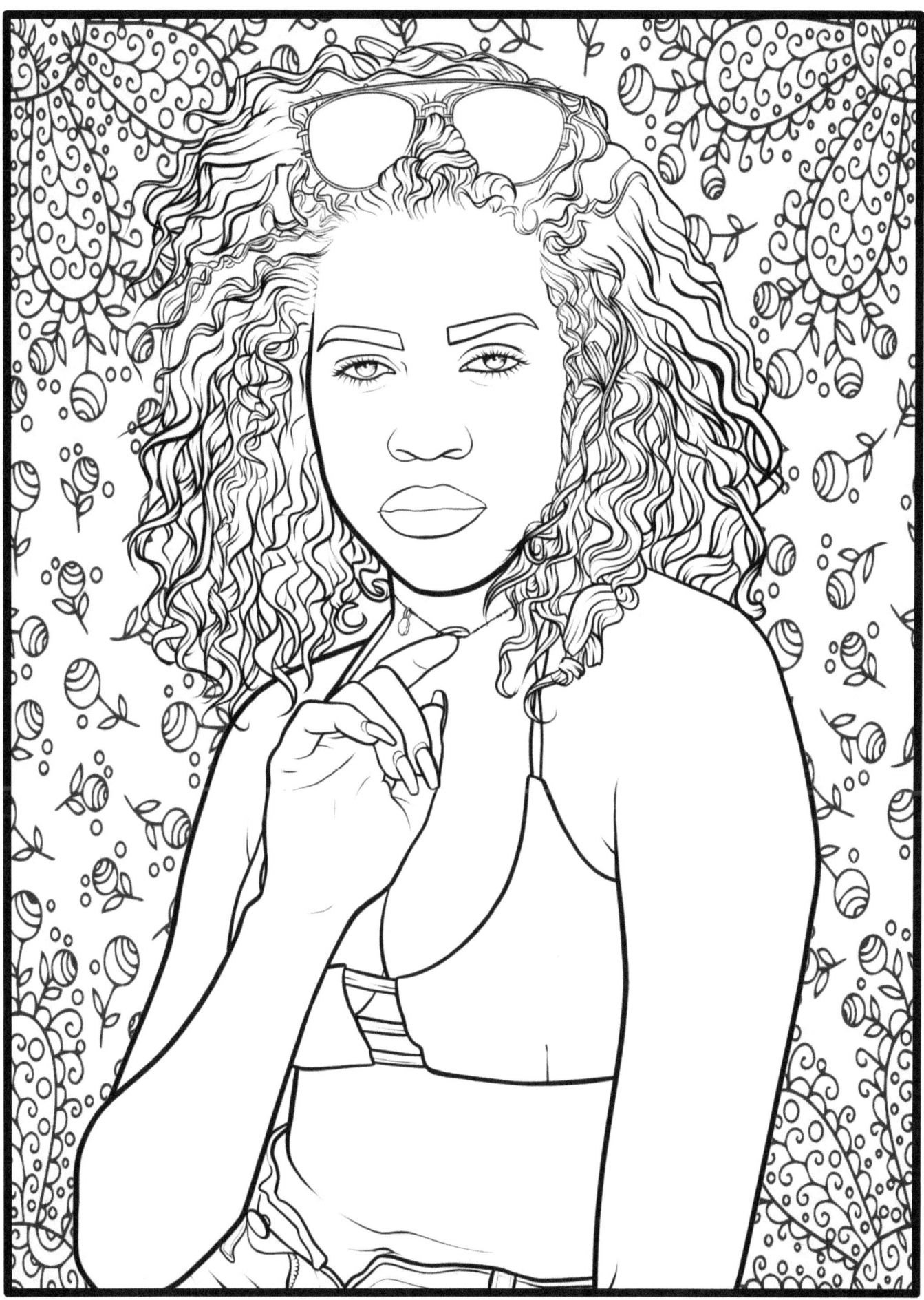

I decided long ago never to walk in anyone's shadow; if I fail, if I succeed, at least I'll live as I believe.
- Whitney Houston

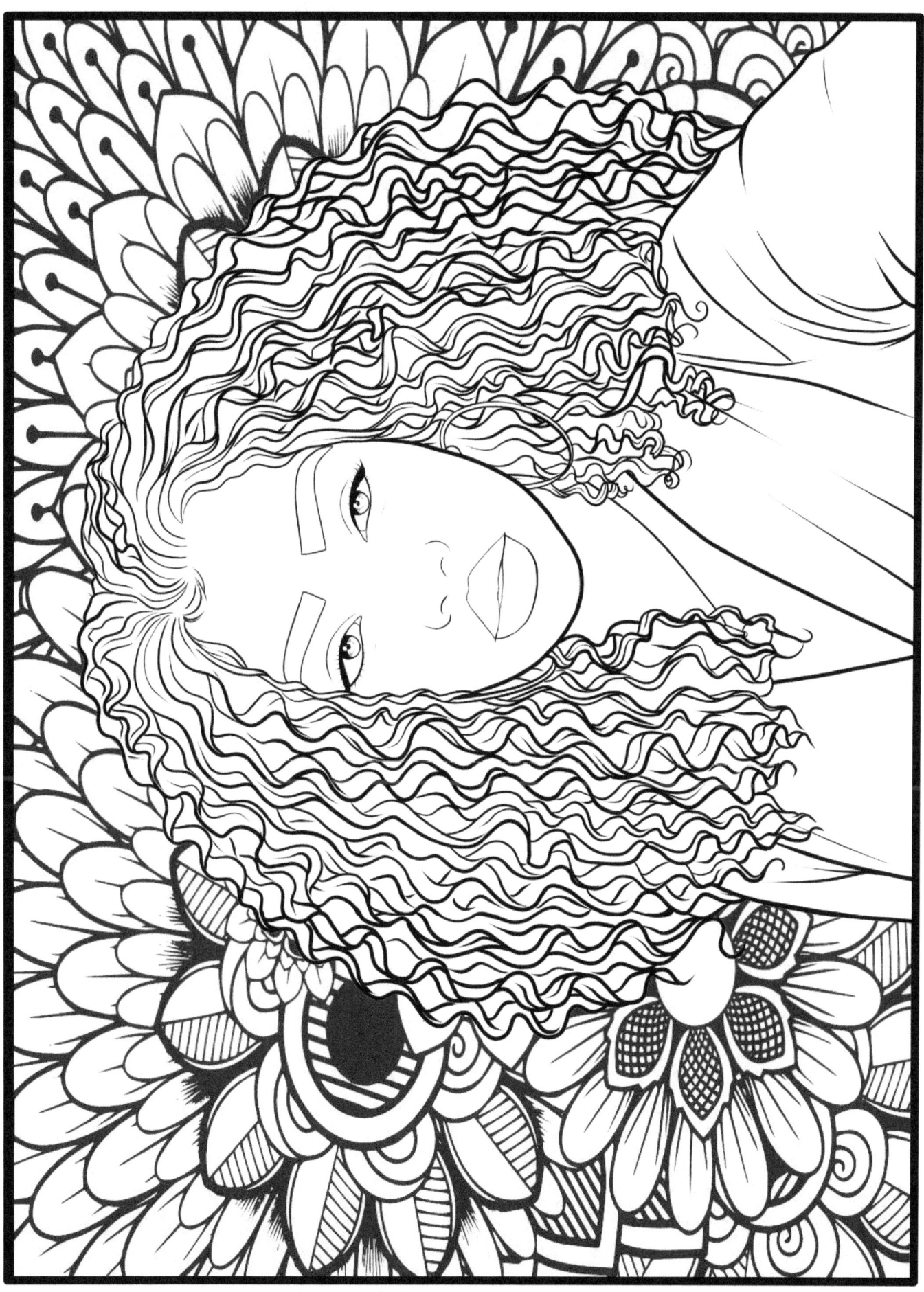

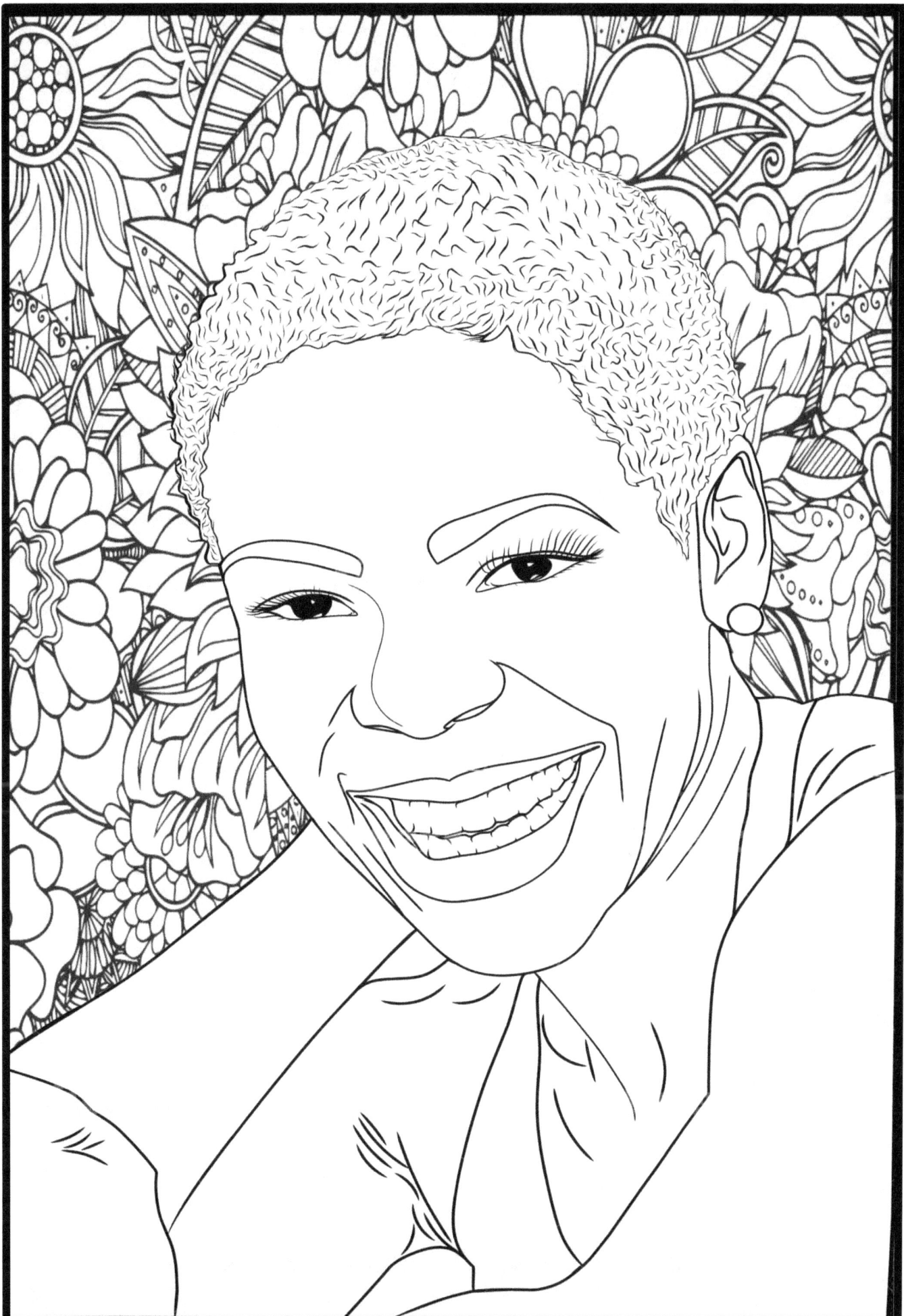

Don't be afraid. Be focused. Be Determined, Be hopeful. Be empowered.
-    Michelle Obama

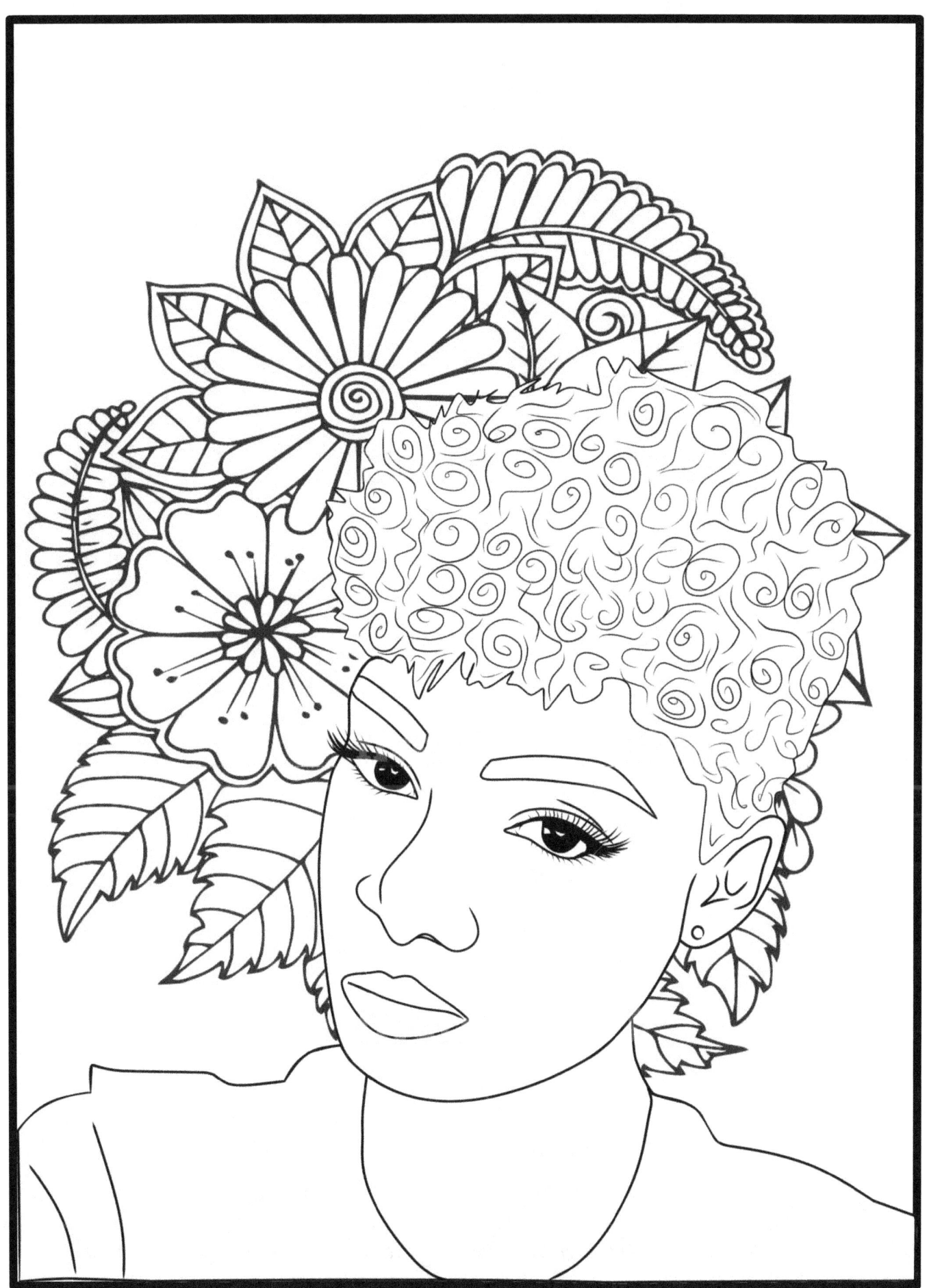

You must never be fearful about what you are doing when it is right.

-    Rosa parks

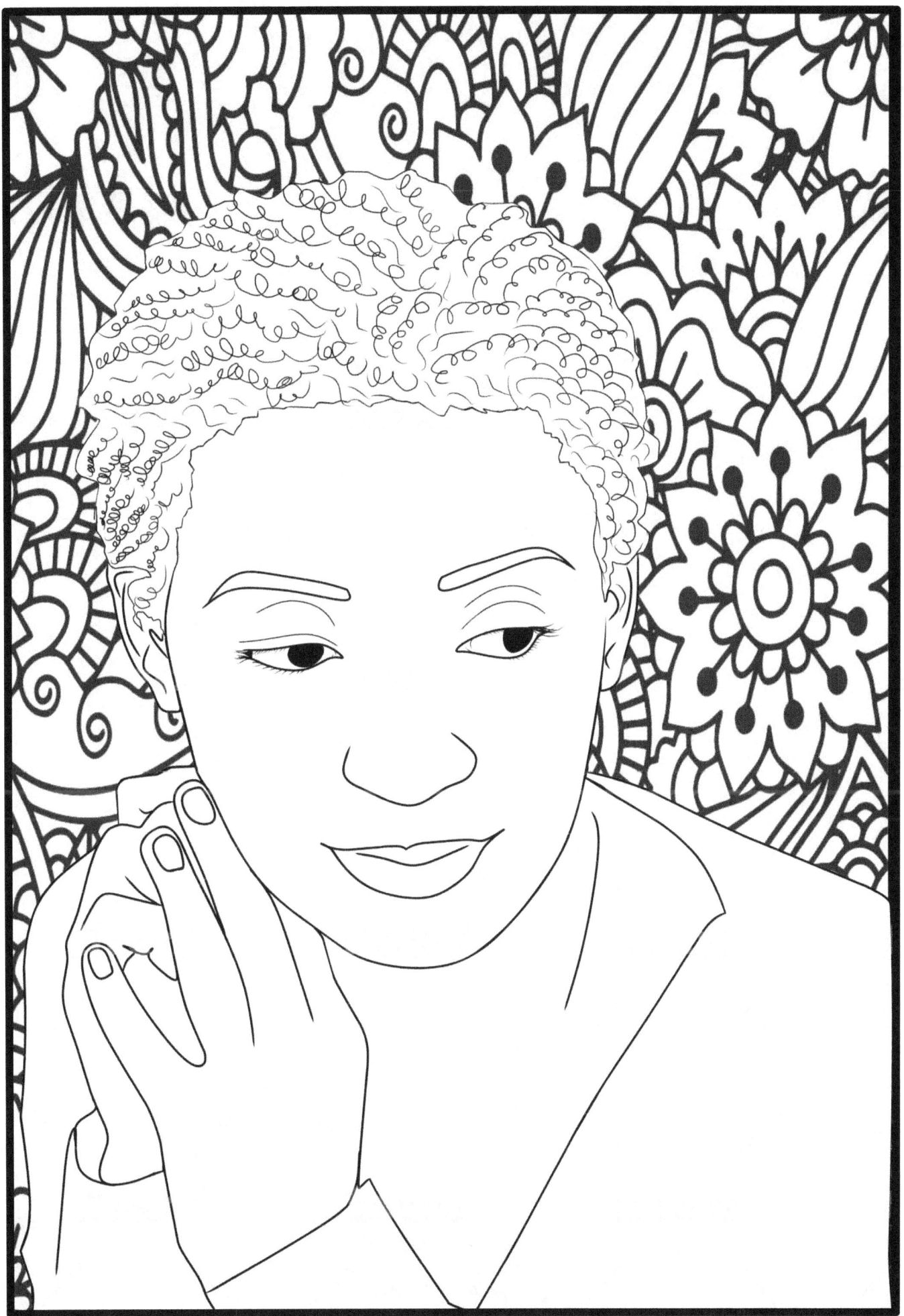

It always seems impossible until it's done.

– Nelson Mandela

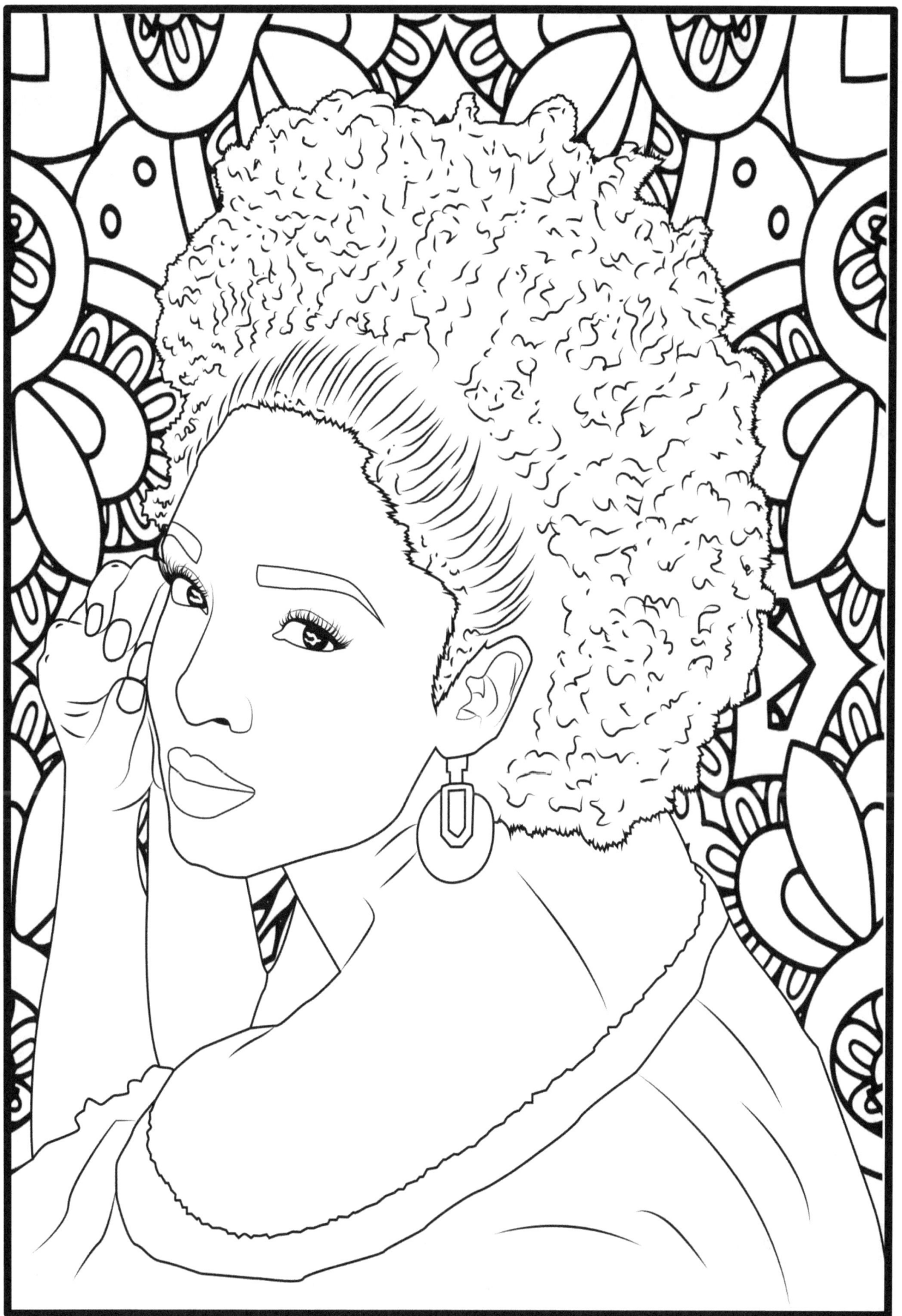

Fail is an important part of your growth and developing resilience. Don't be afraid to fail.

-    Michelle Obama

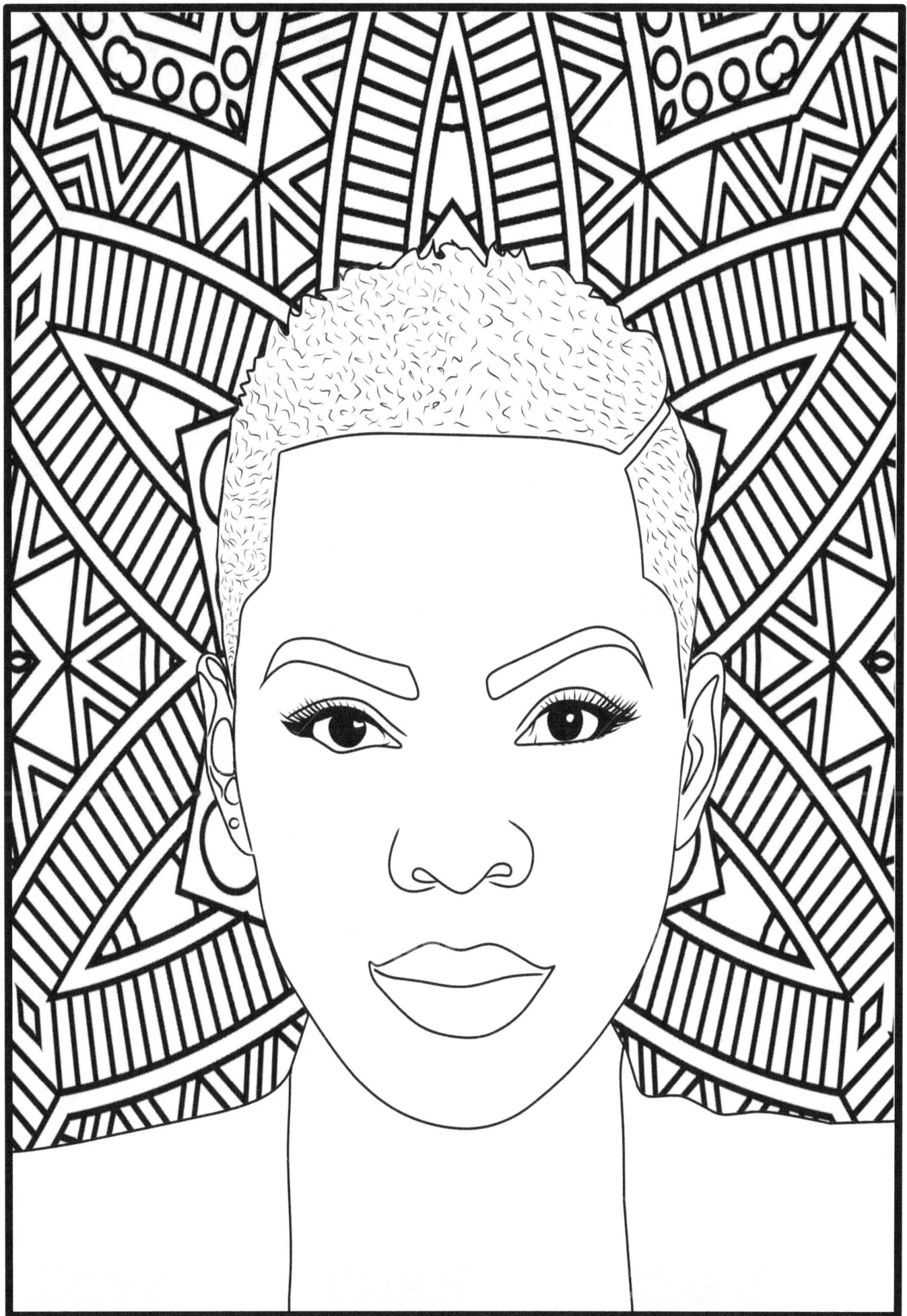

I will not let anyone walk through my mind with their dirty feet.

-Mahatma Gandhi

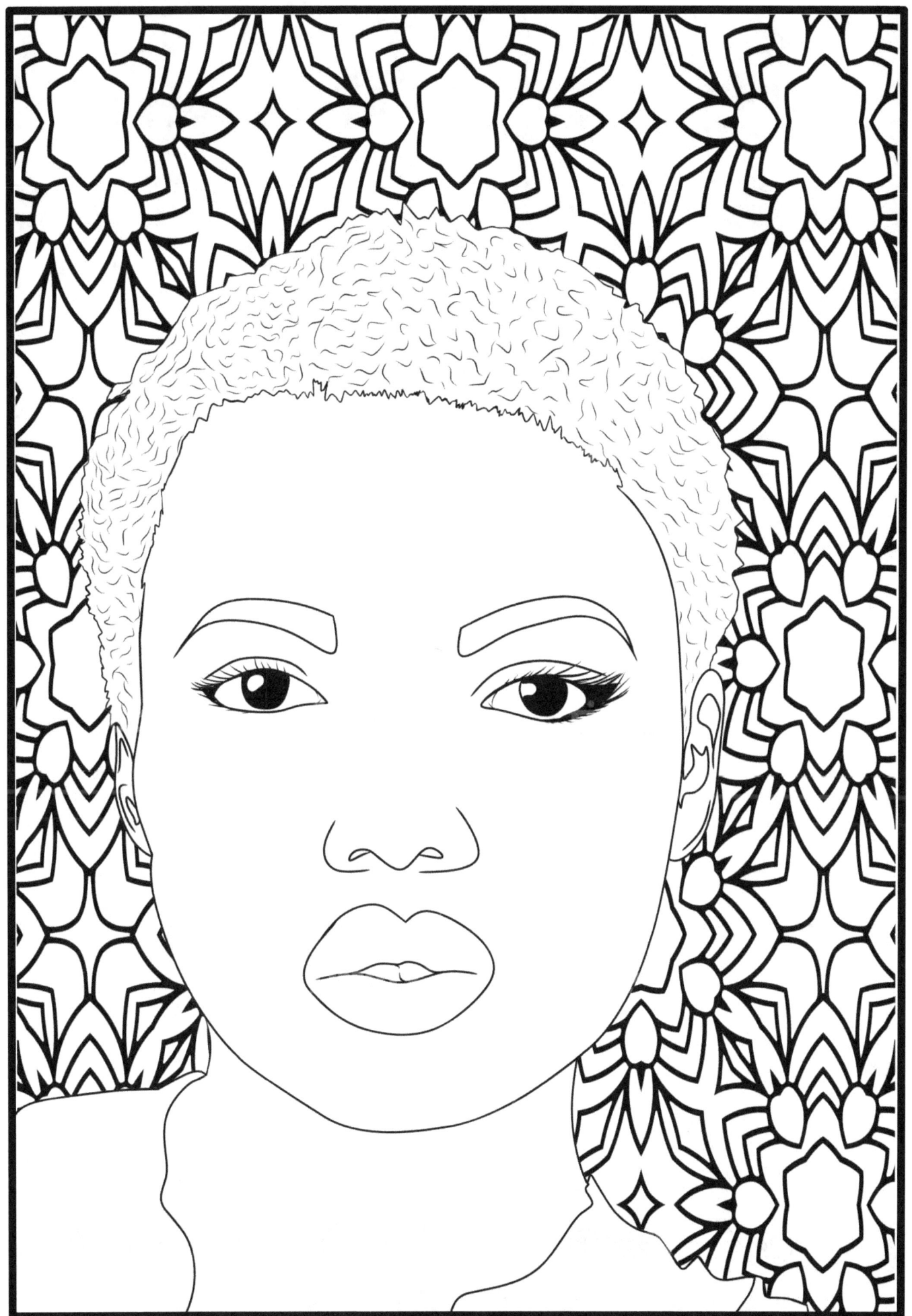

If you do not tell the truth about yourself you cannot tell it about other people.

– Virginia Wolf

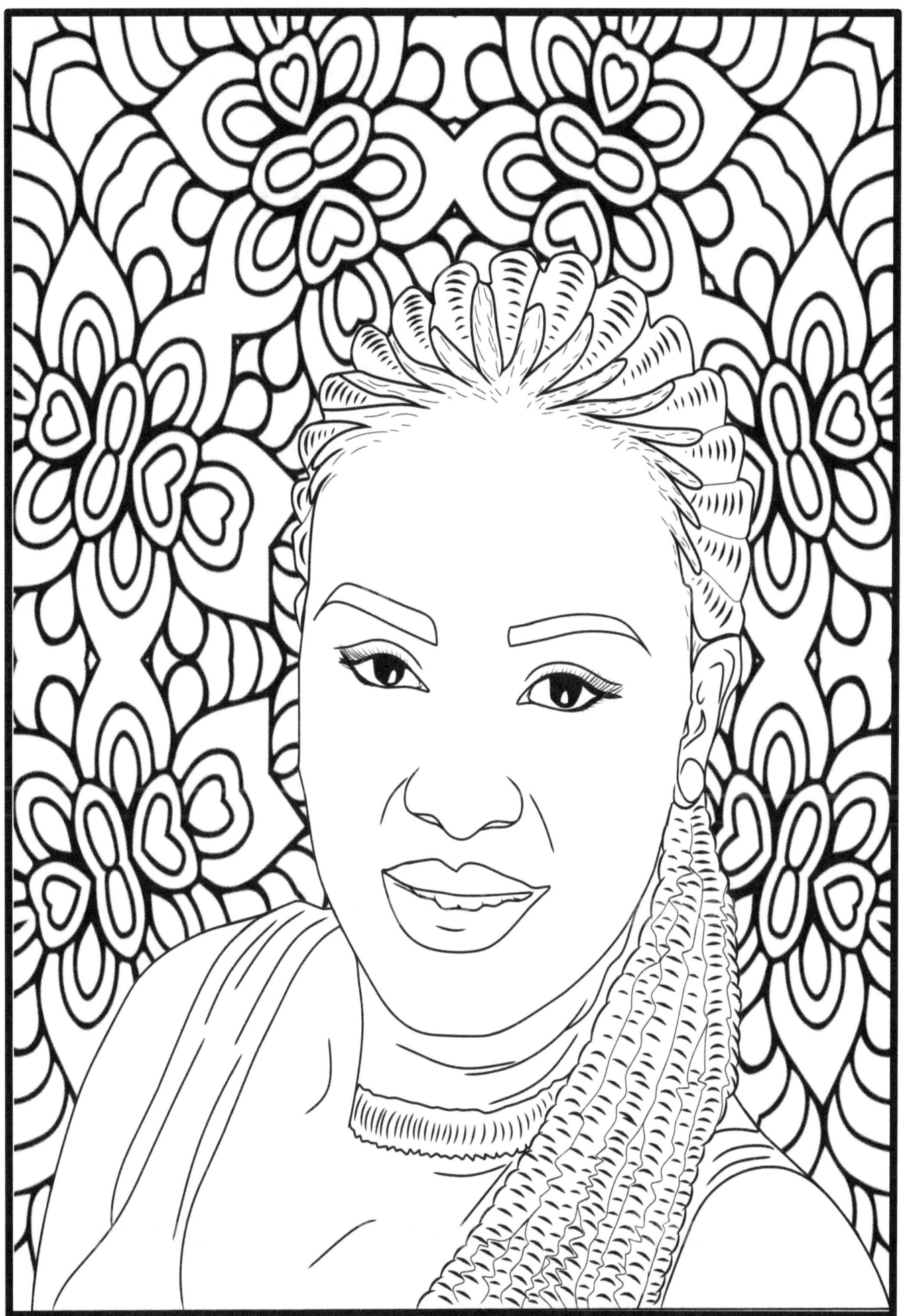

It is not the load that breaks you down, it's the way you carry it.

– Lena Horne

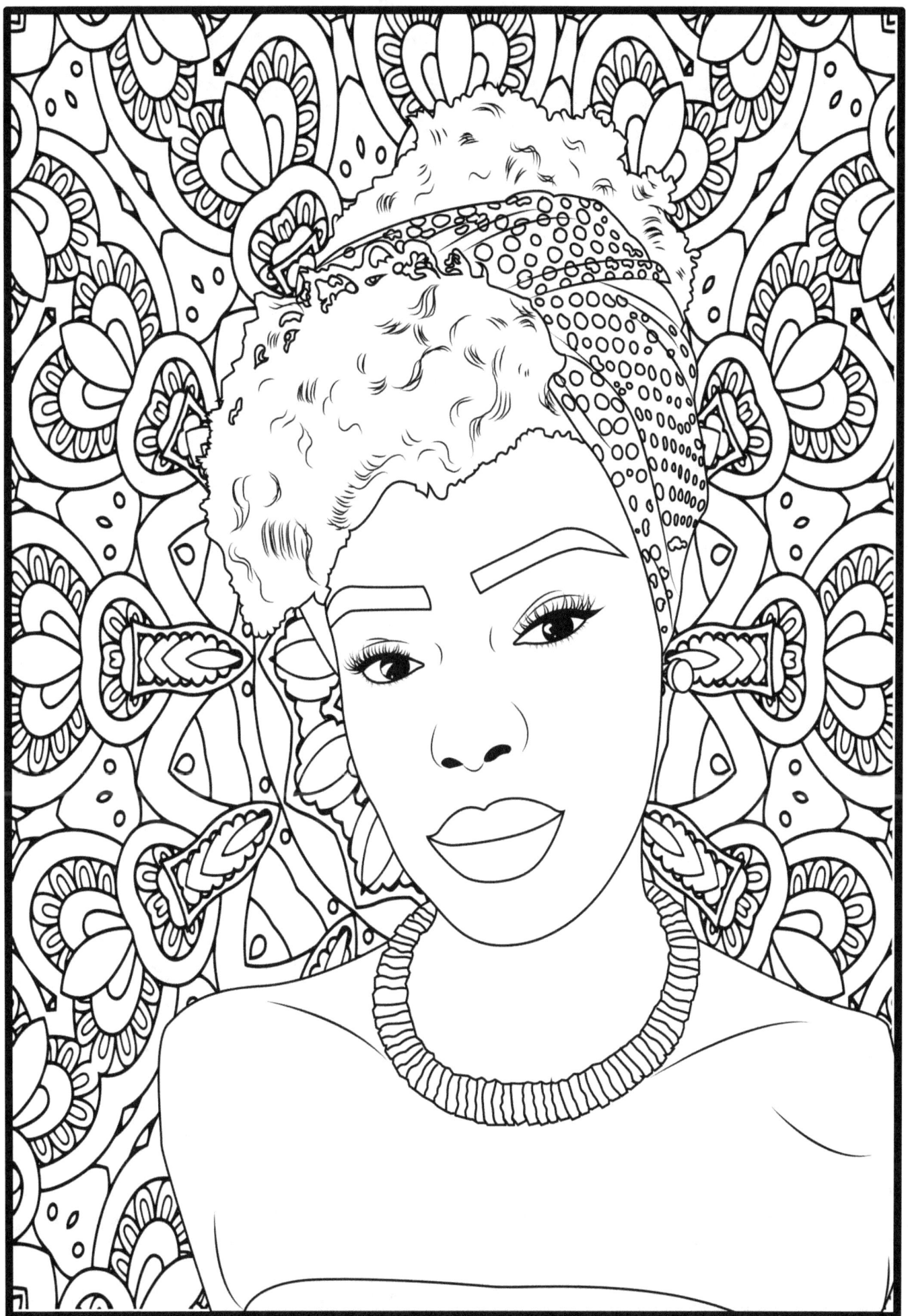

Challenges make you discover things about yourself that you never really knew. They're what make the instrument stretch, what make you go beyond the norm.

- Cicely Tyson

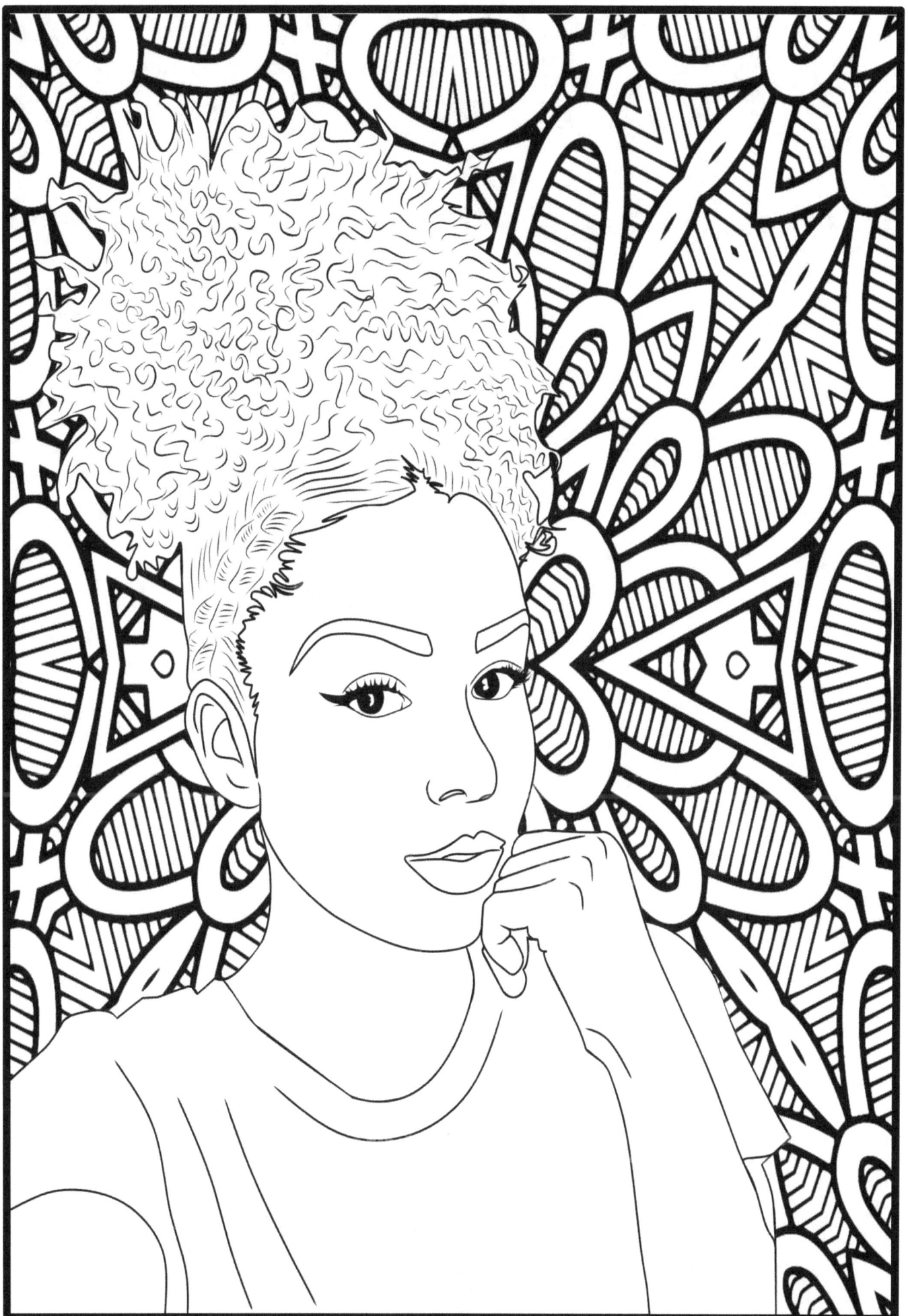

The time is always right to do the right thing.

- Dr. Martin Luther King JR

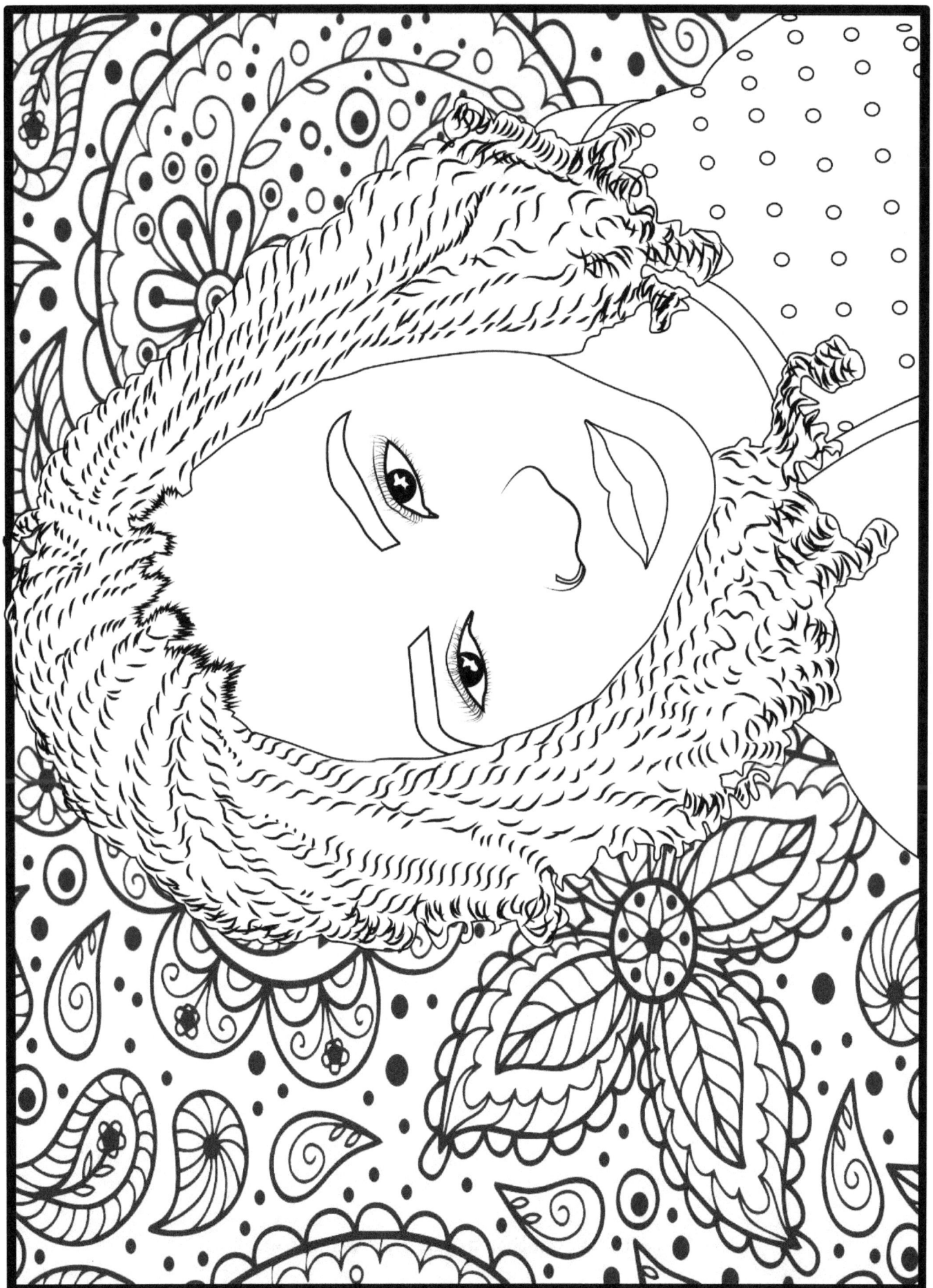

Normal is nothing more than a cycle on a washing machine.

– Whoopi Goldberg

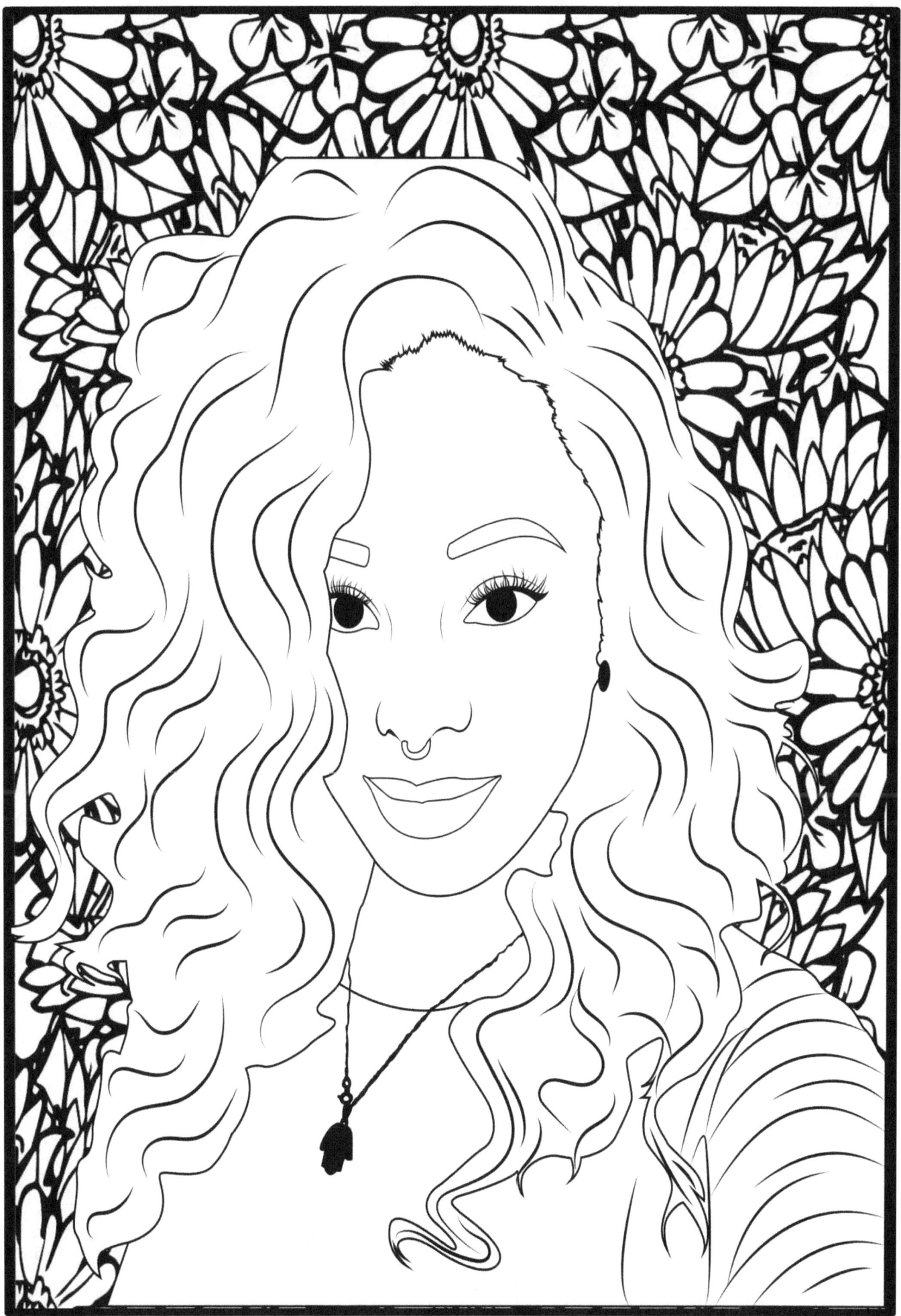

Nothing will work unless you do.

- Dr. Maya Angelou

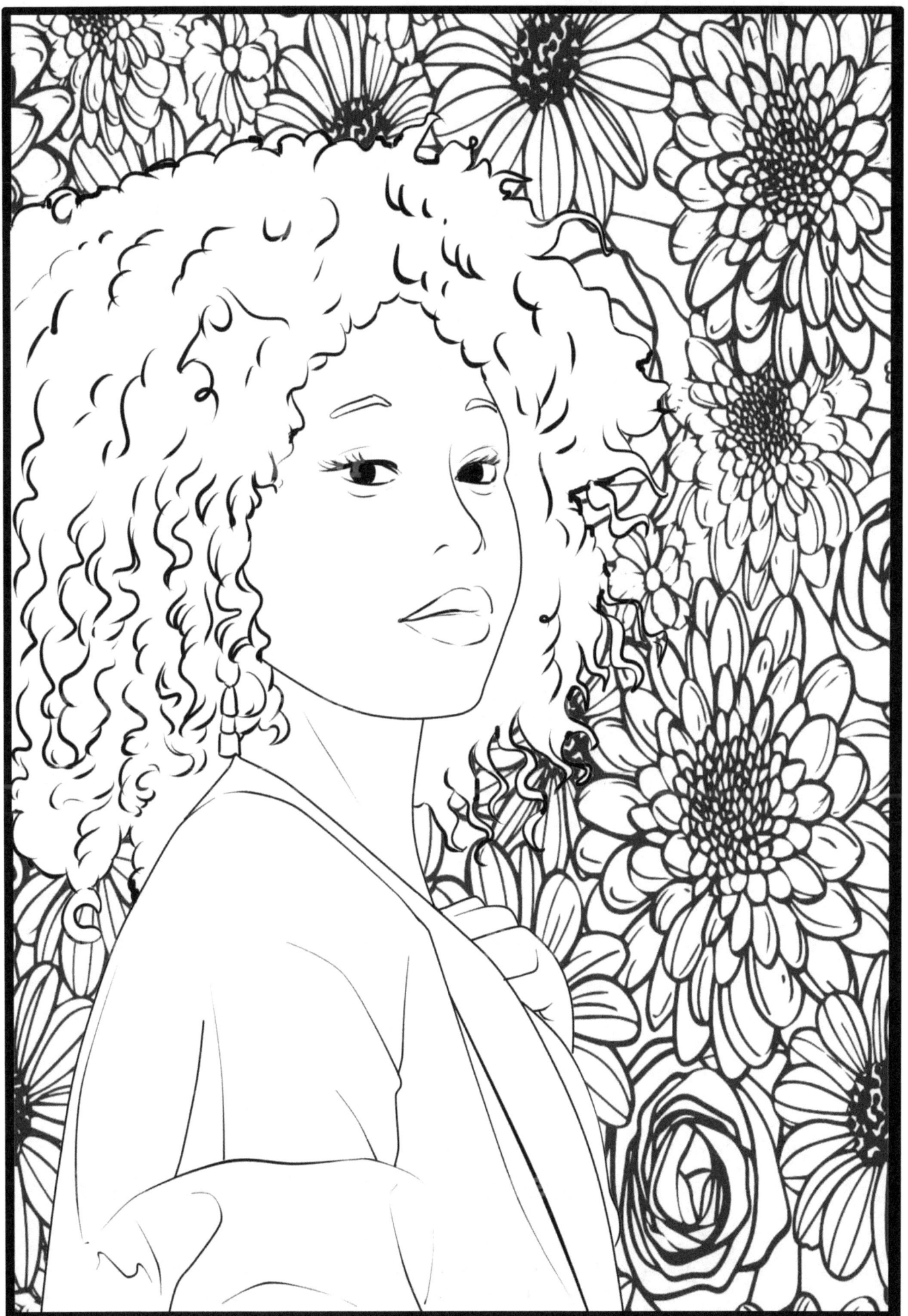

When people show you who they are, believe them.
- Dr. Maya Angelou

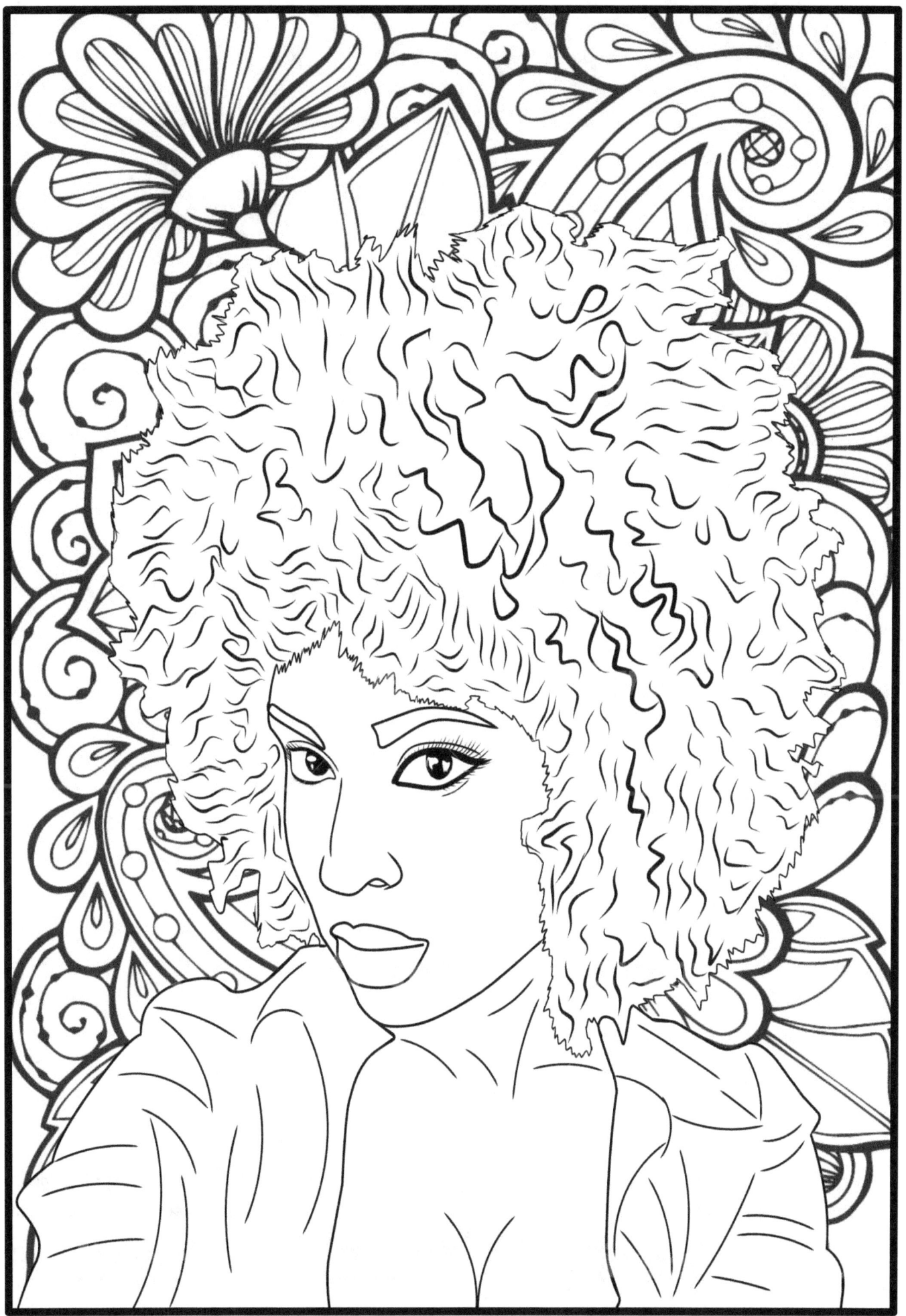

I hope that my presence on your screen and my face in magazines may lead you young girls, on a beautiful journey. That you will feel the validation of your external beauty, but also get to the deeper business of being beautiful inside.

– Lupita Nyong'o

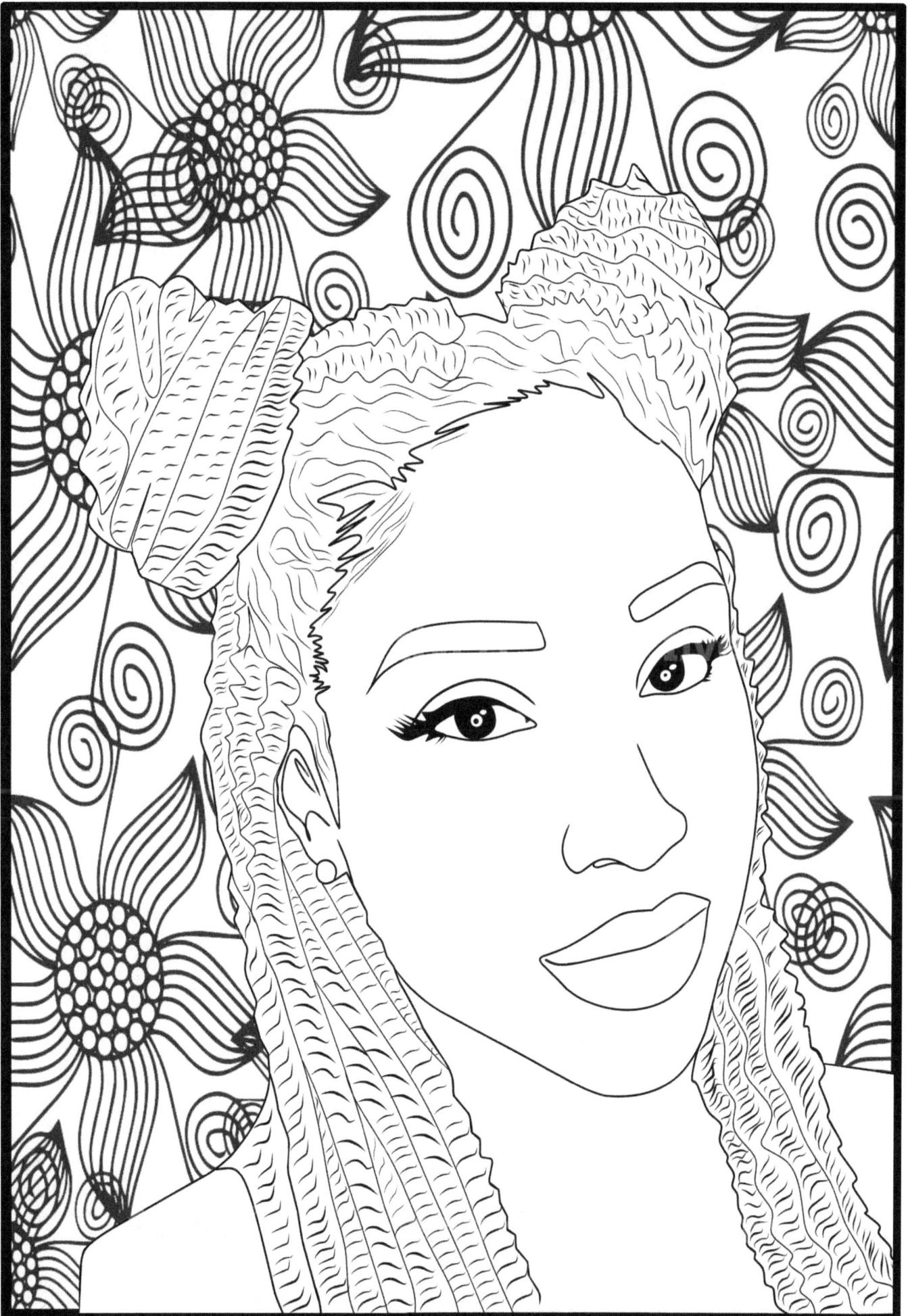

Your self-worth is determined by you. You don't have to depend on someone telling you who you are.

– Beyonce

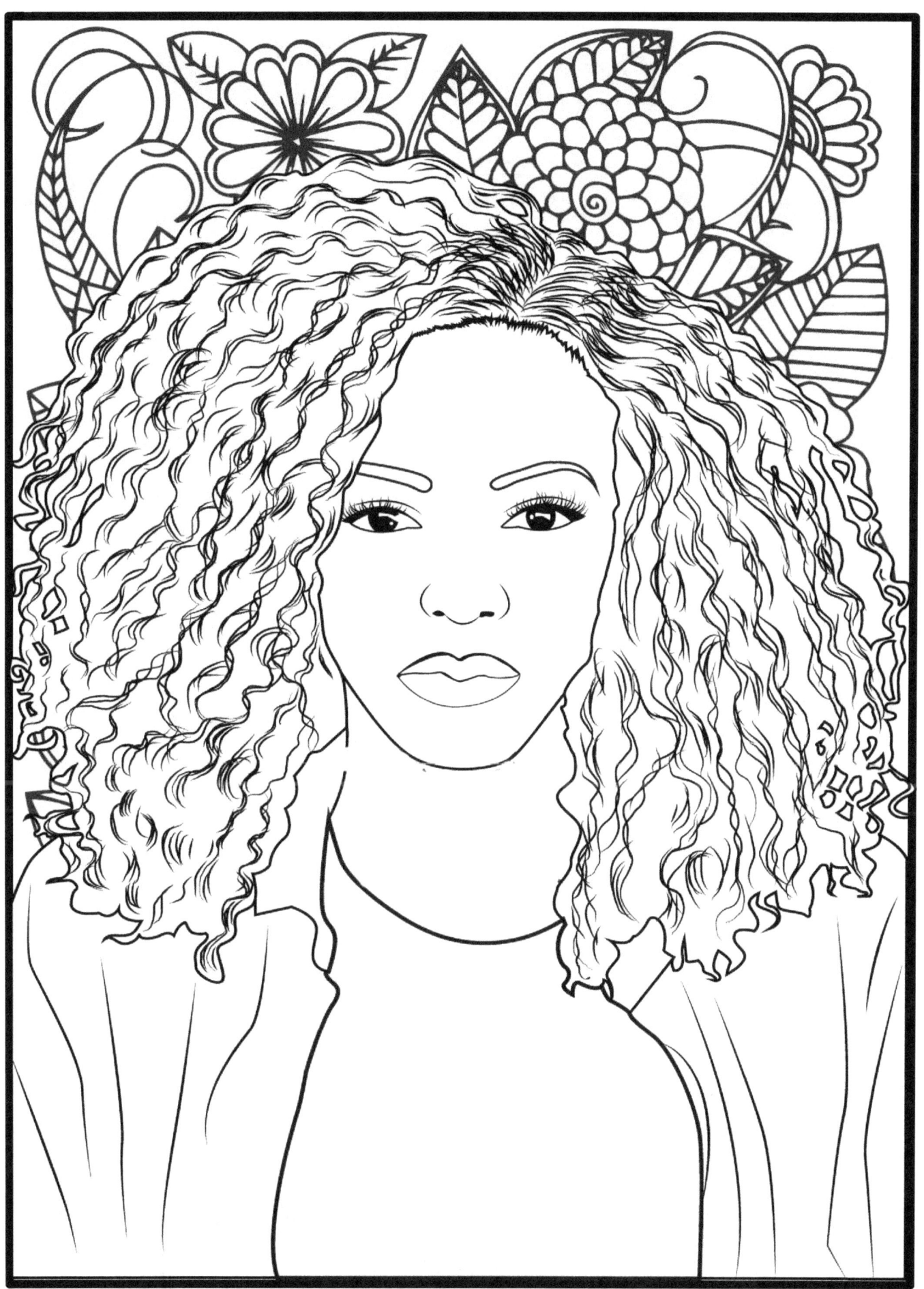

Fight for the things you care about, but do it in a way that will lead others to join you.

– Ruth Bader Ginsburg

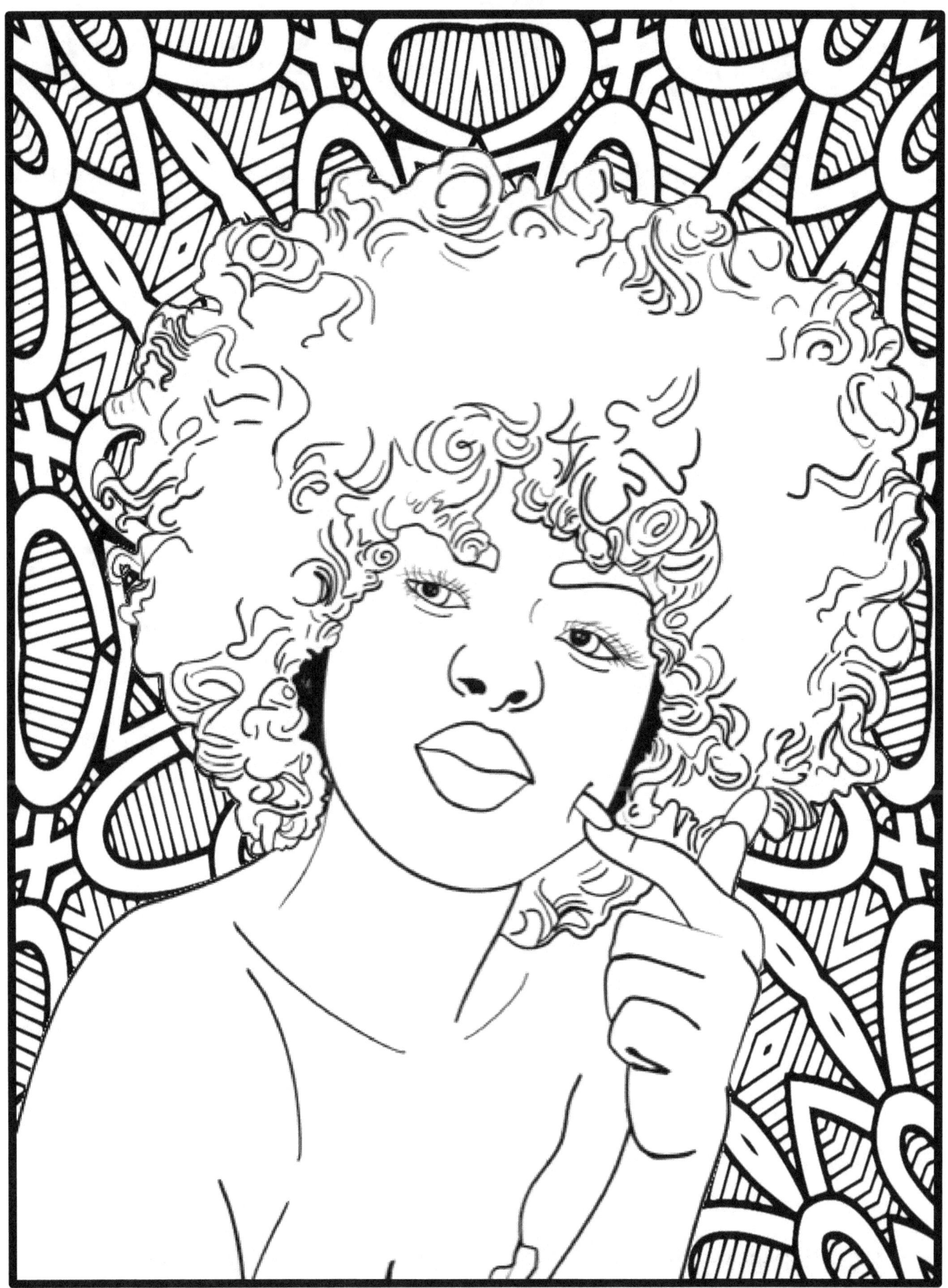

If you cannot fine peace within yourself, you will never find it anywhere else.

– Marvin Gaye

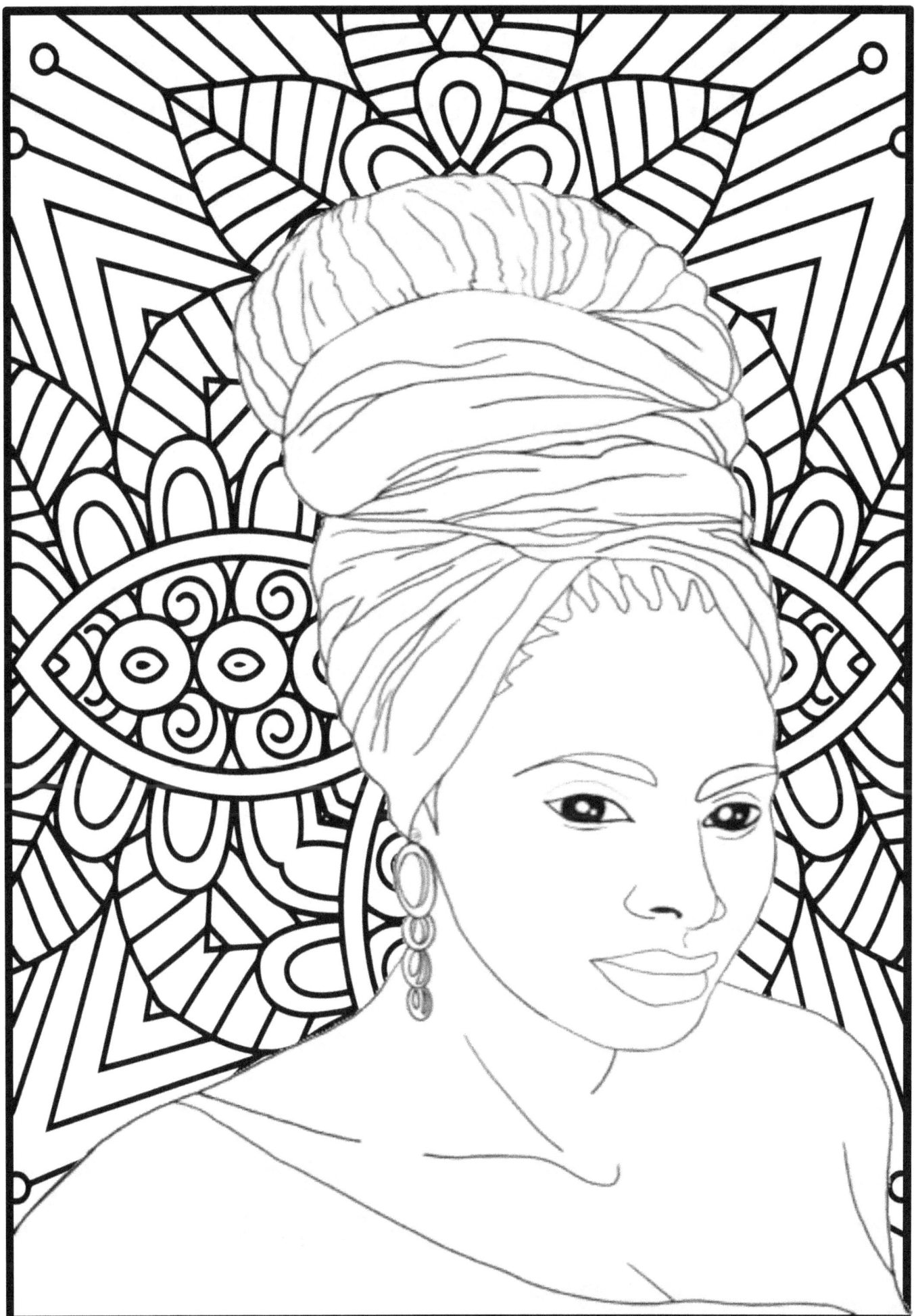

Be hopeful. Be Optimistic. Never lose that sense of hope.

-John Lewis

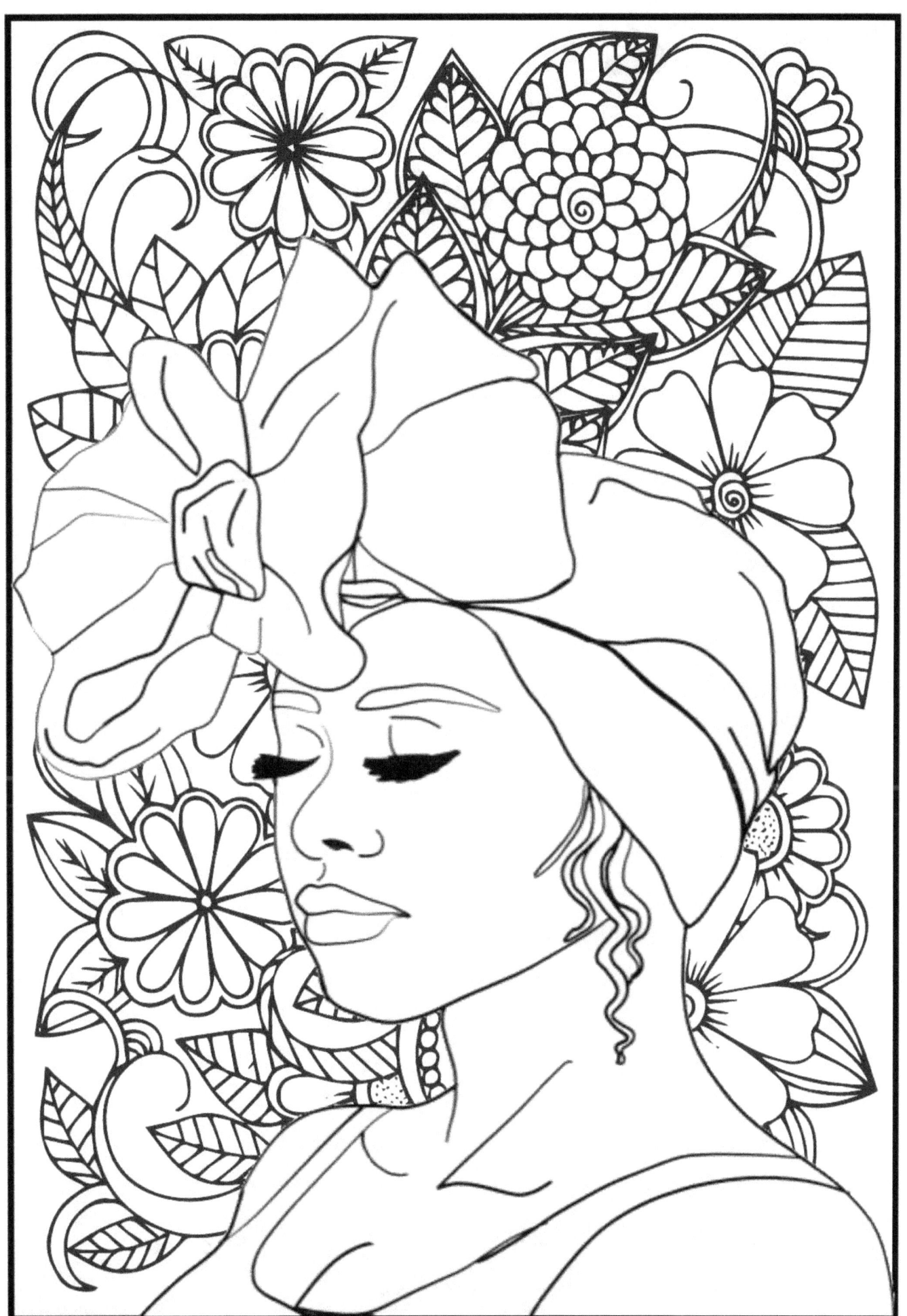

Success is liking yourself, liking what you do, and liking how you do it.

– Dr. Maya Angelou

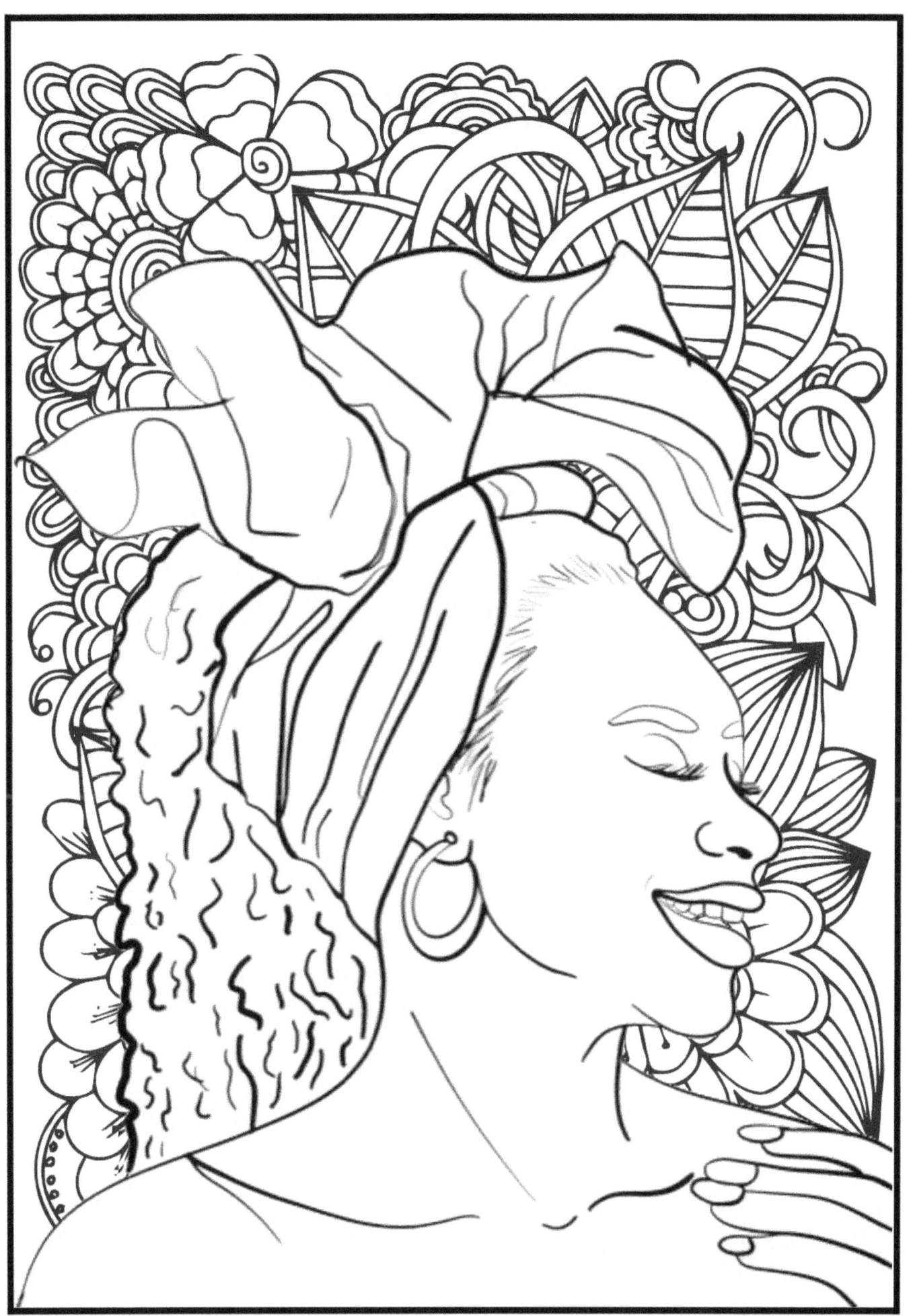

I never cared much for what people SAY. What I am interested in is what they DO.

– Shirley Chisholm

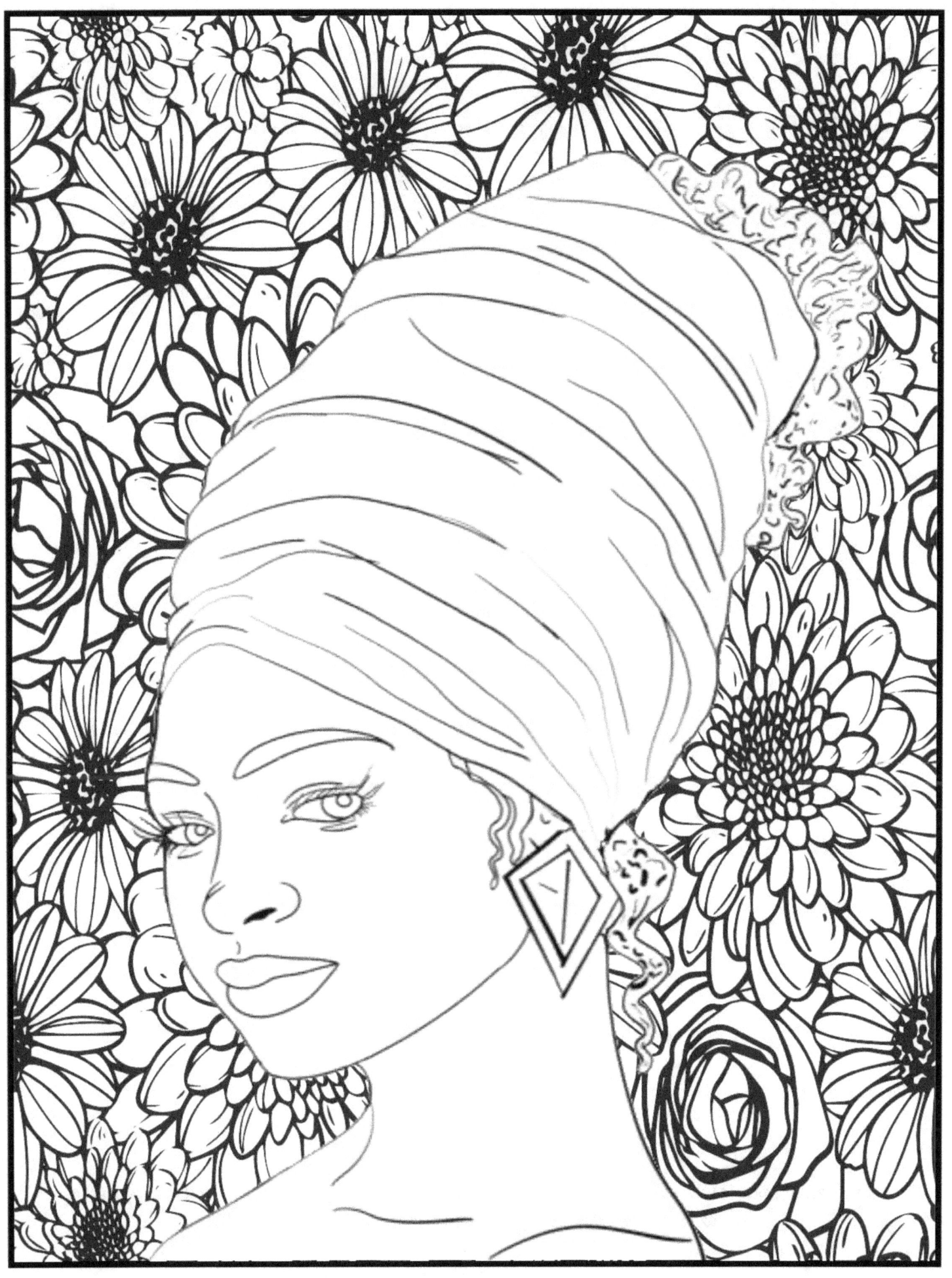

Through life people will make you mad, disrespect you and treat you bad. Let God deal with the things they do, because hate in your heart will consume you too.

– Will Smith

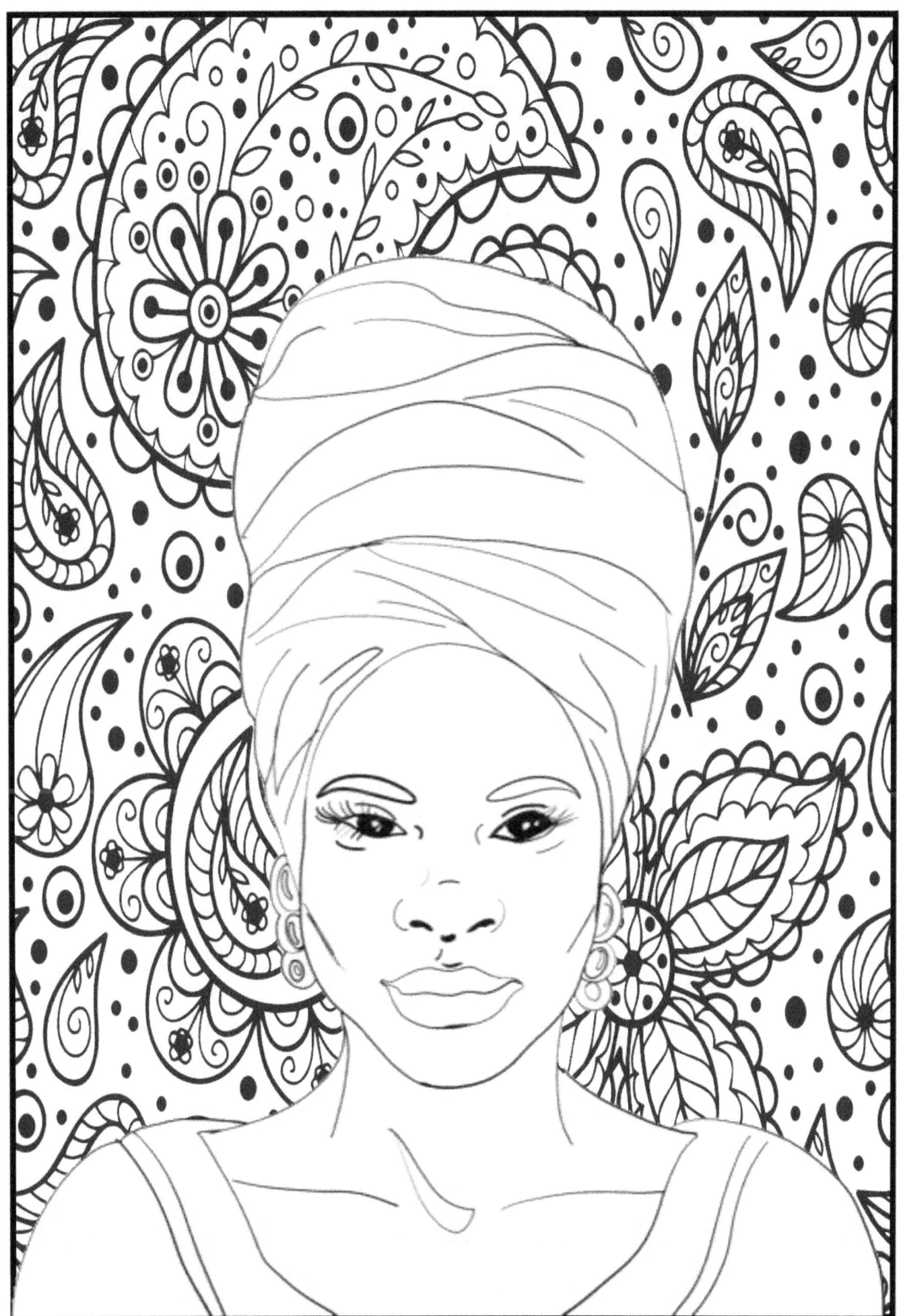

I am no longer accepting the things I cannot change. I am changing the things I cannot accept.

– Angela Davis

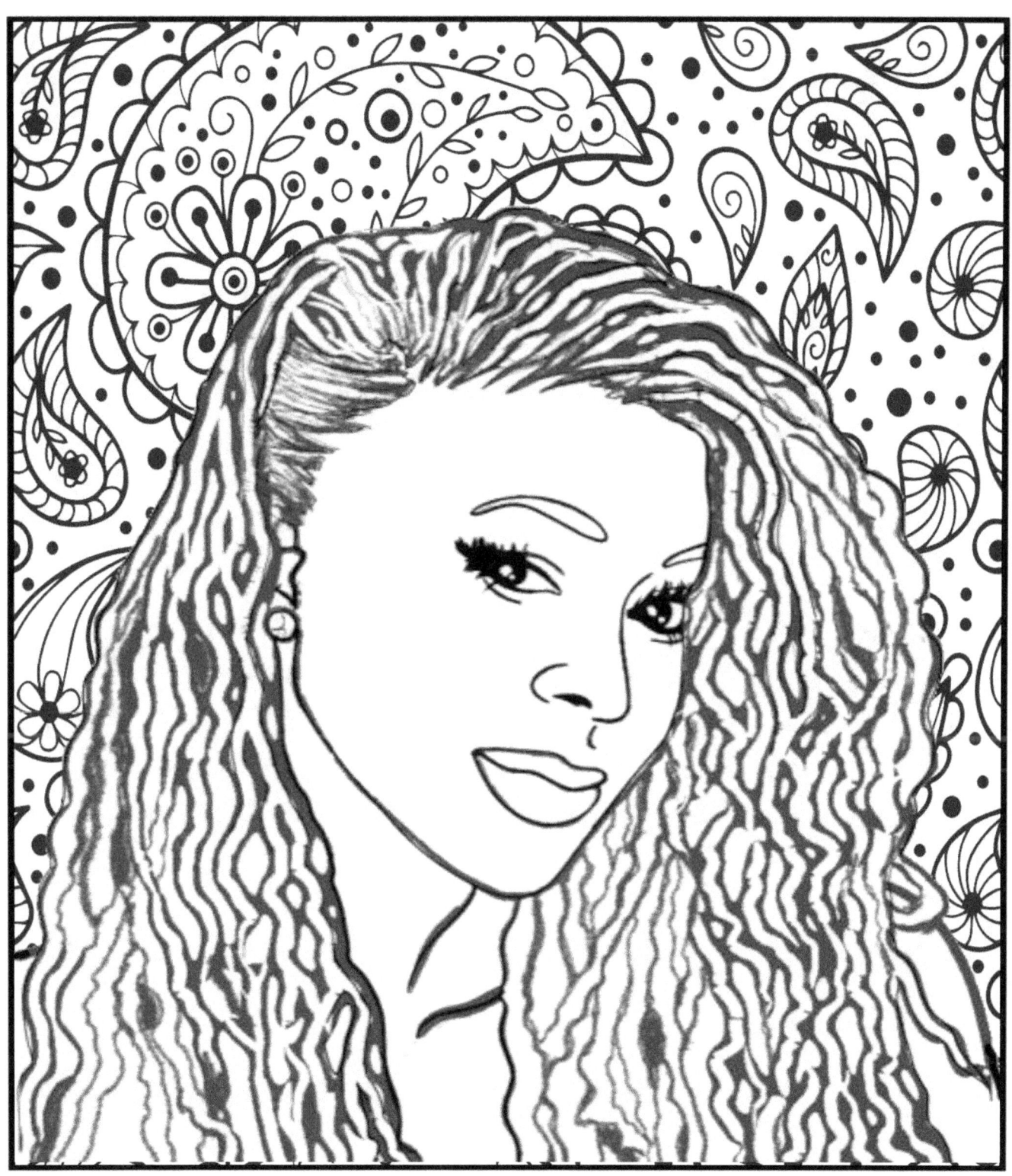

Respect yourself enough to walk away from anything that no longer serves you, grows you, or makes you happy.

-    Robert Tew

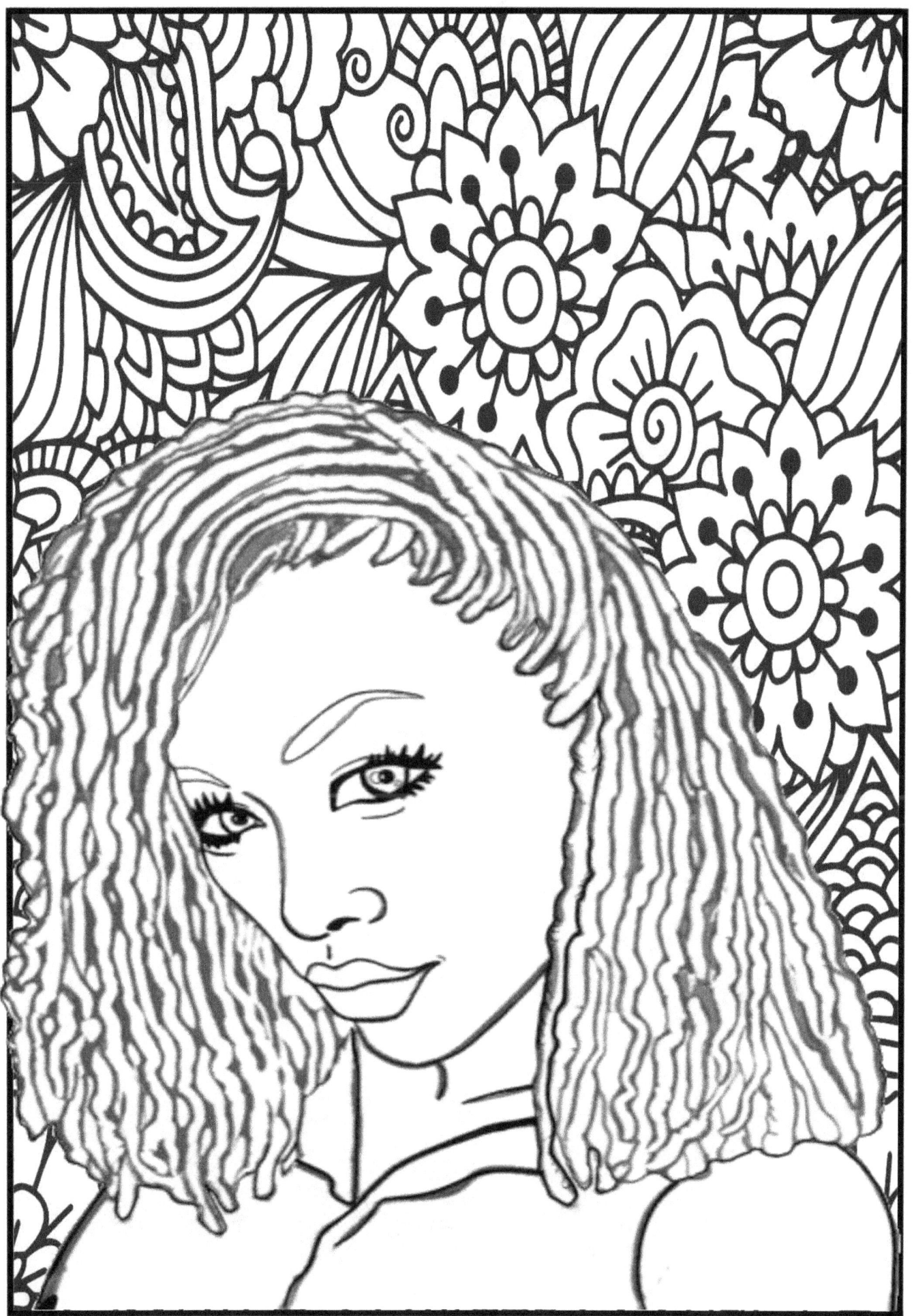

Always be yourself, express yourself, have faith in yourself, do not go out and look for a successful personality and duplicate it.

- Bruce Lee

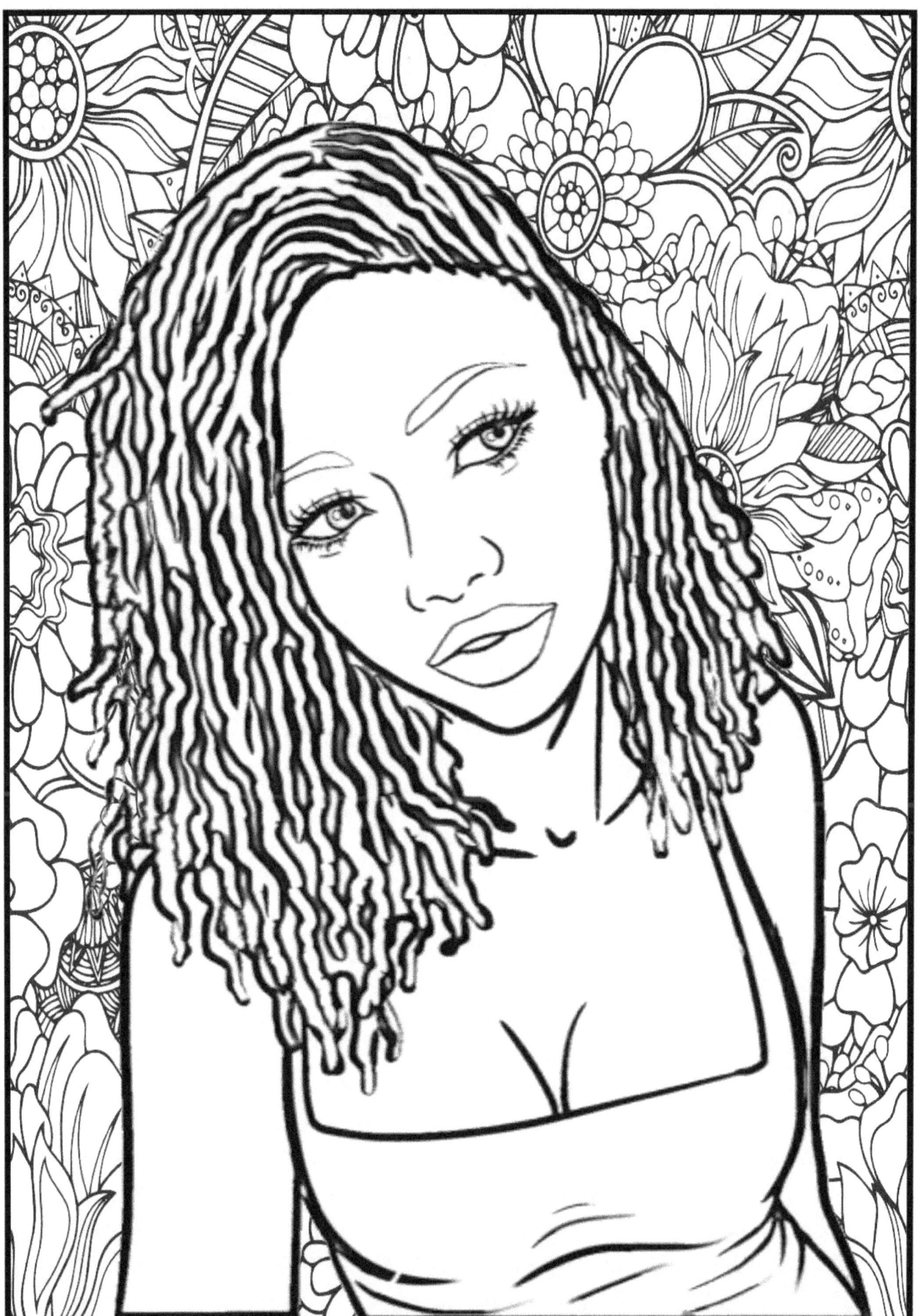

Every relationship you have is a reflection of your relationship with yourself.

- Deepak Chopra

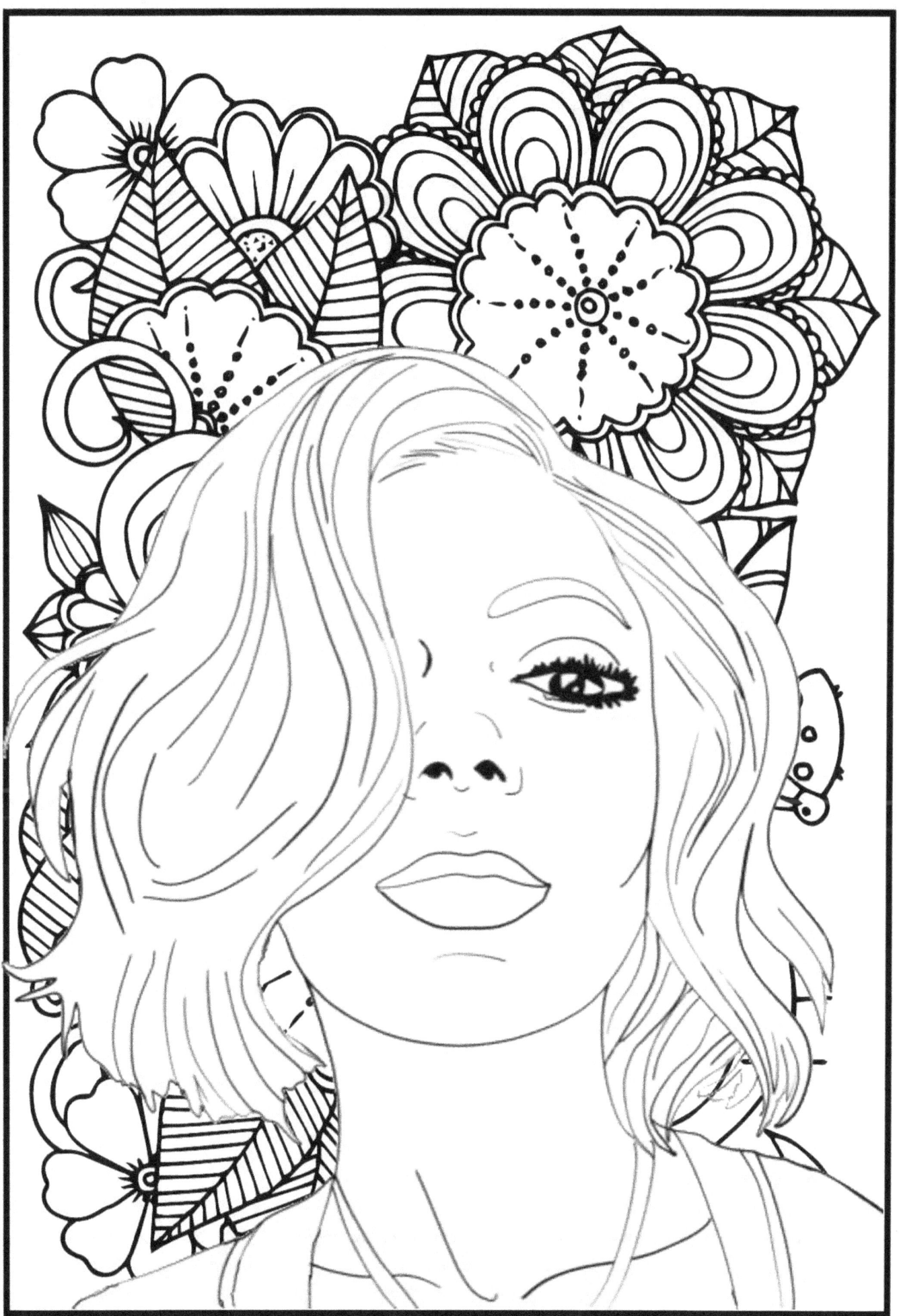

Action is a great restorer and builder of confidence. Inaction is not only the result but the cause, of fear.
— Norman Vincent Peale

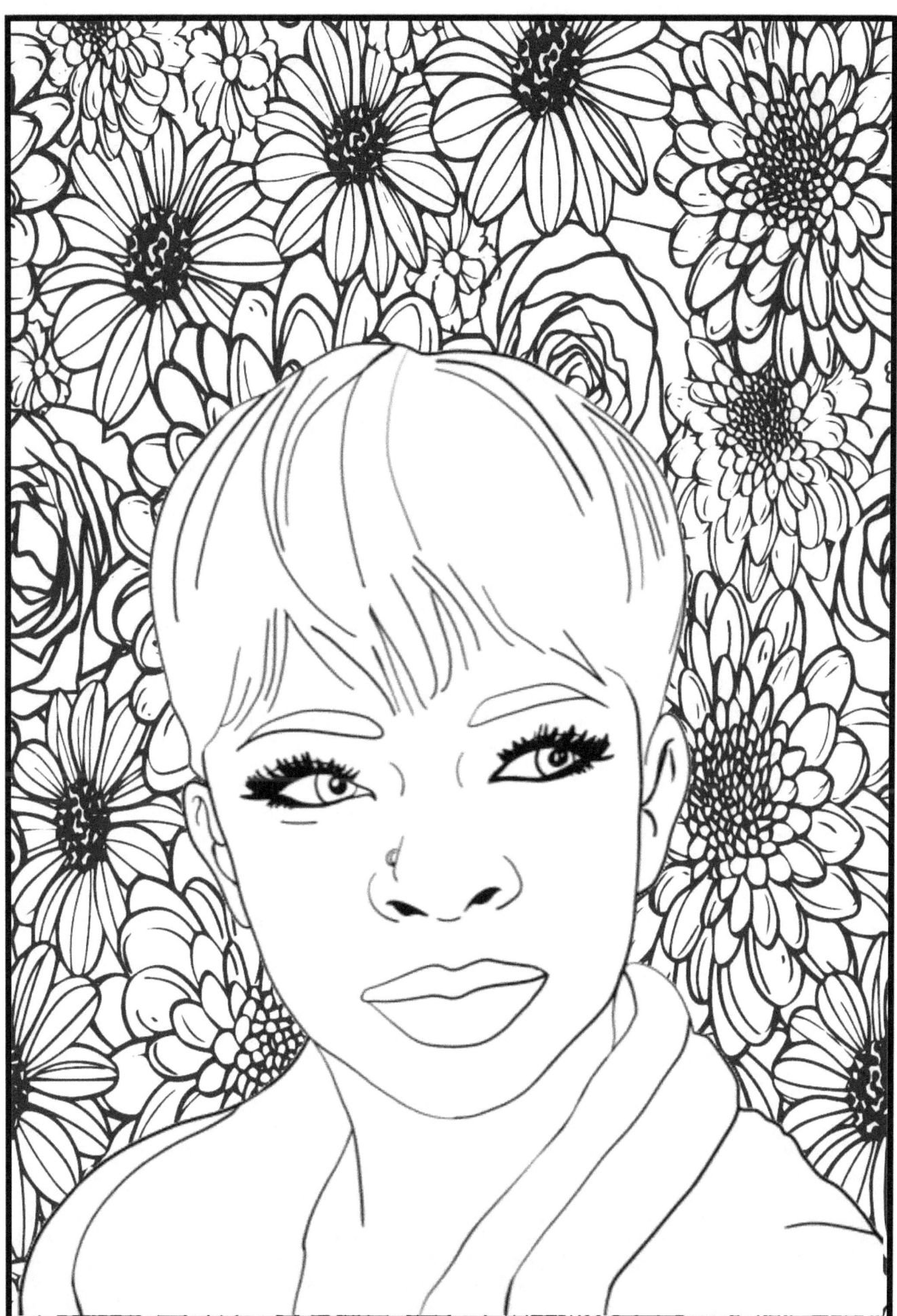

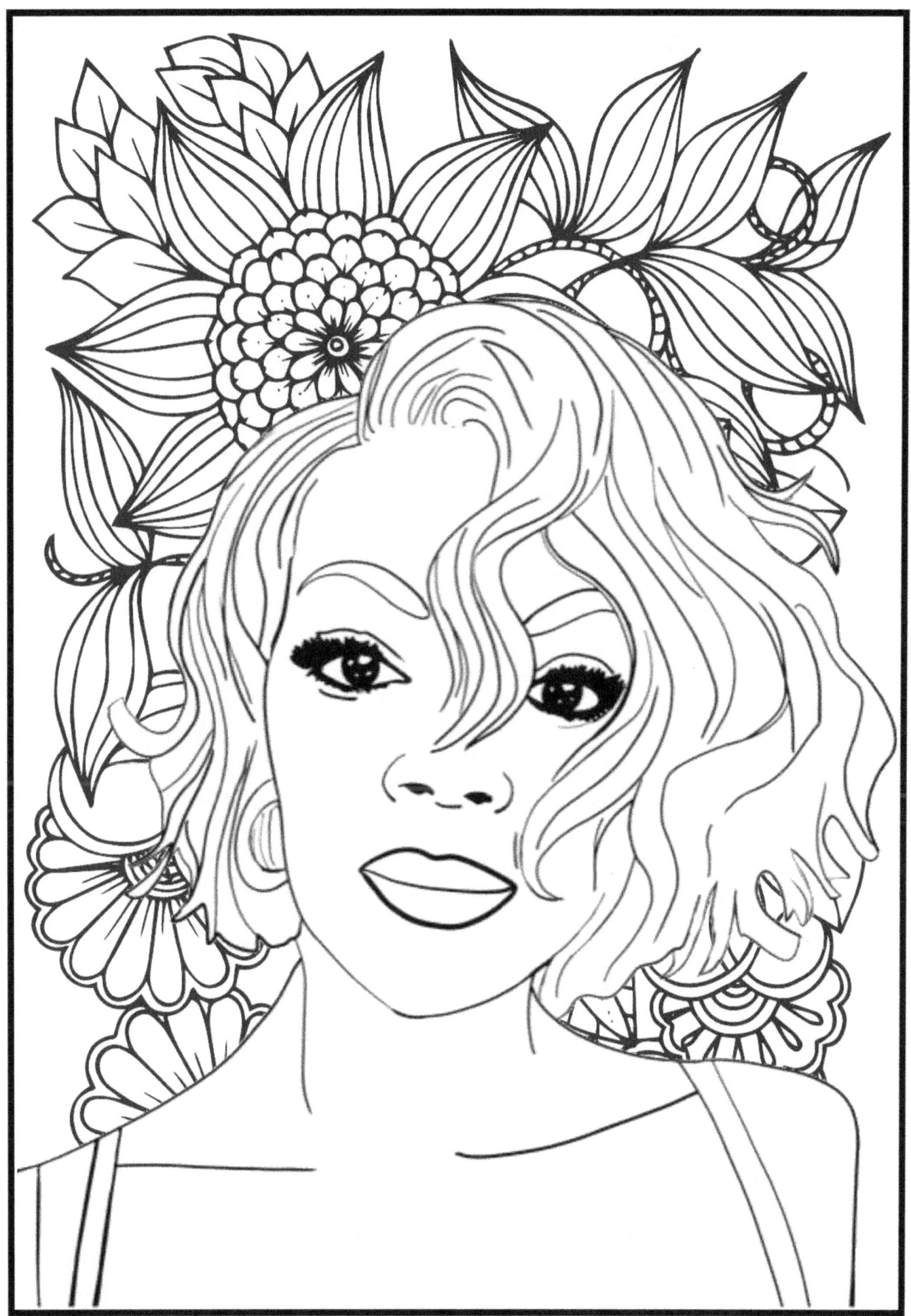

Life is not easy for any of us. But what of that? We must have perseverance and above all confidence in ourselves. We must believe that we are gifted for something and that this thing, at whatever cost, must be attained.
– Marie Curie

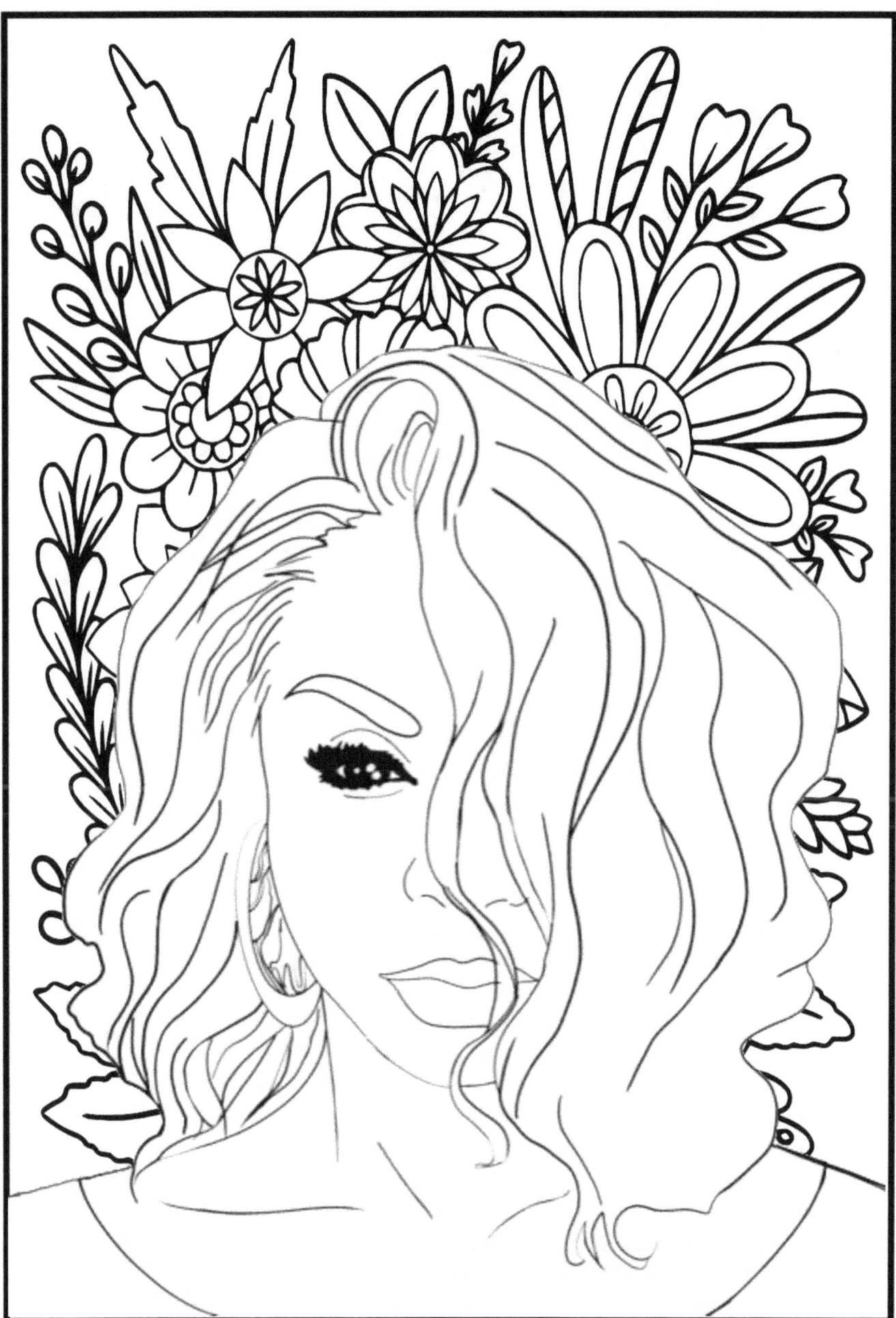

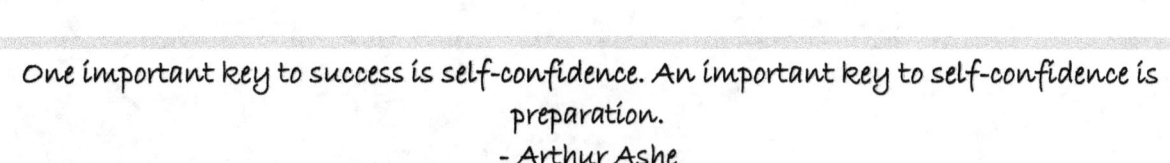
One important key to success is self-confidence. An important key to self-confidence is preparation.
- Arthur Ashe

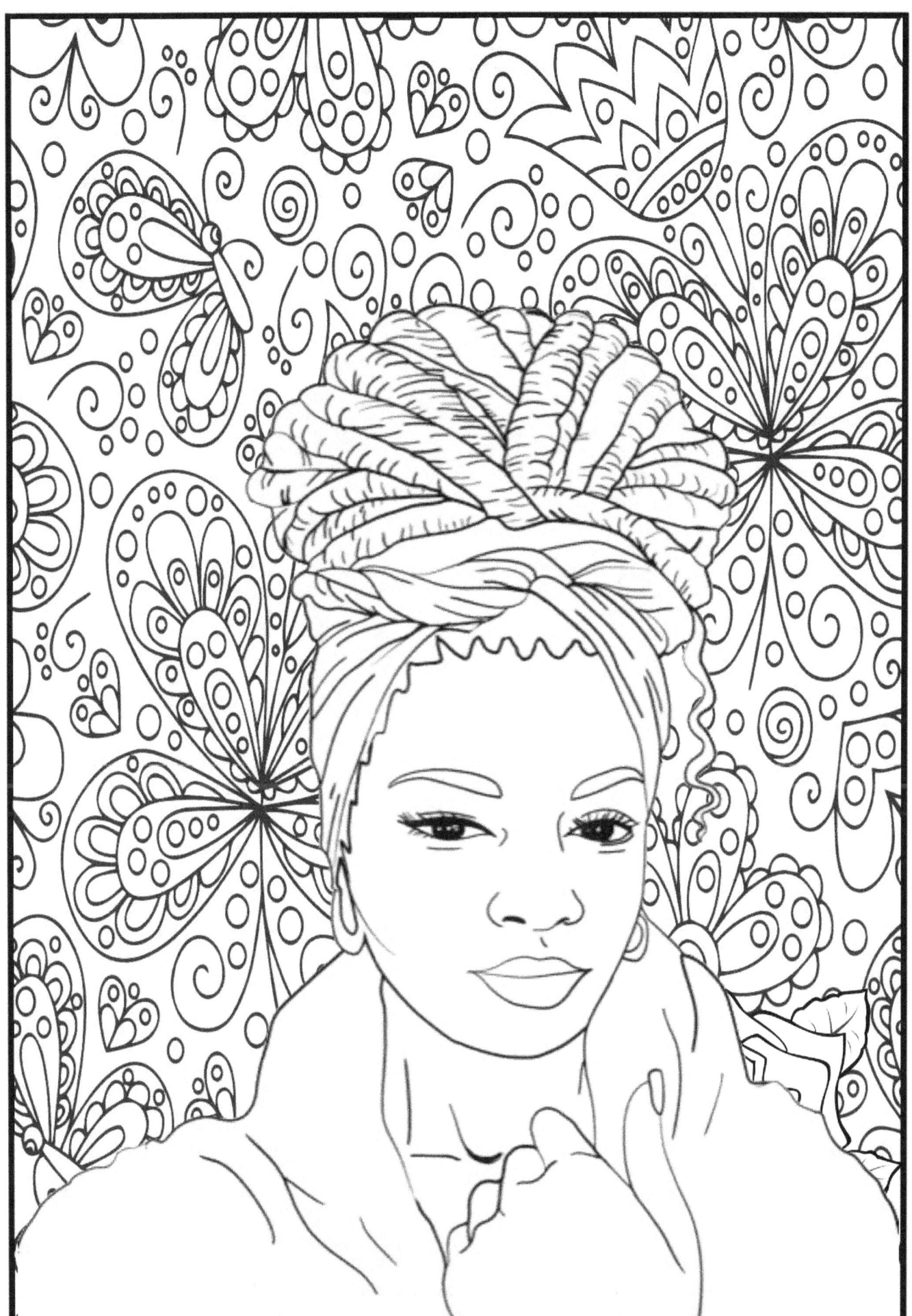

No one can make you feel inferior without your consent. – Eleanor Roosevelt

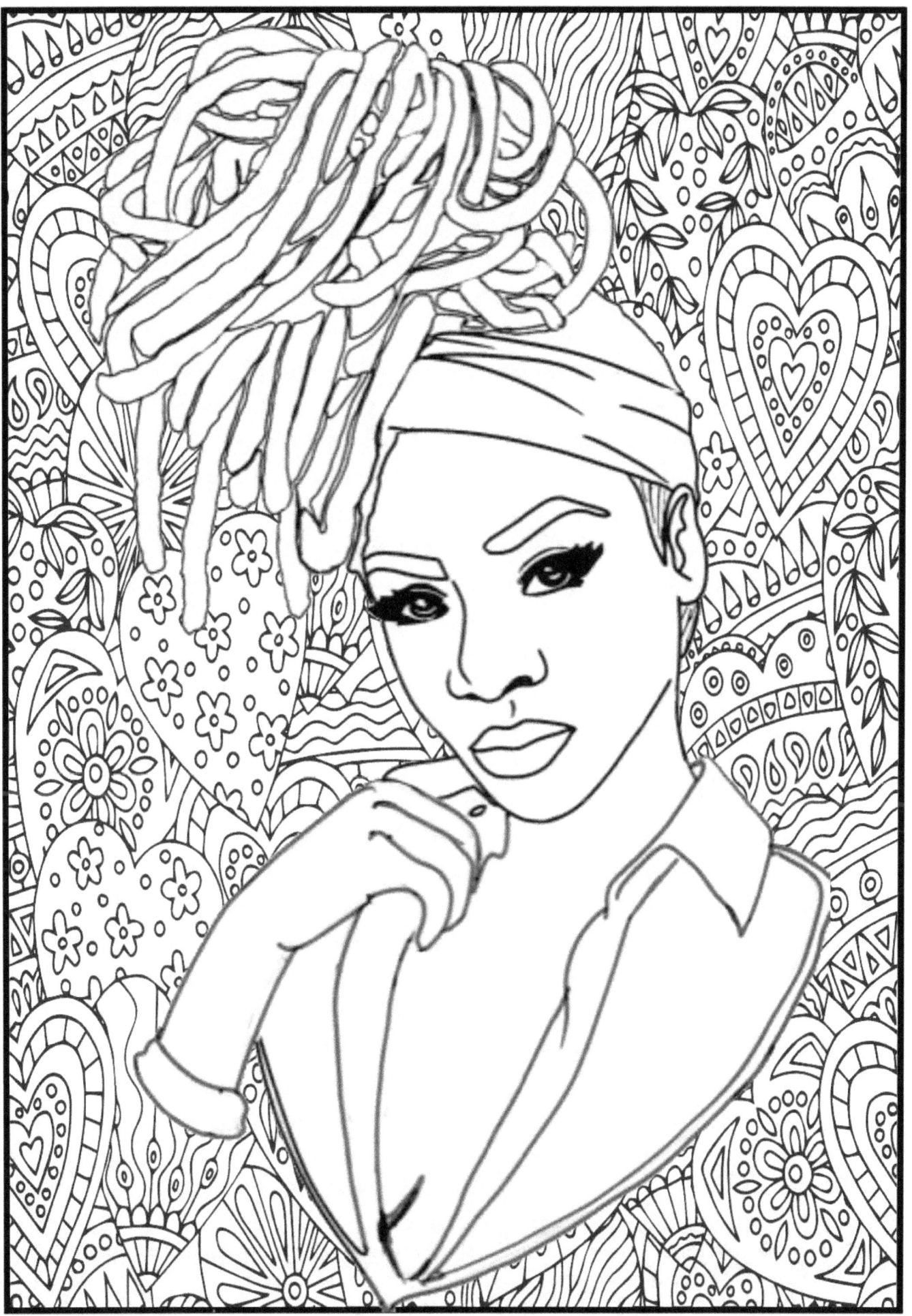

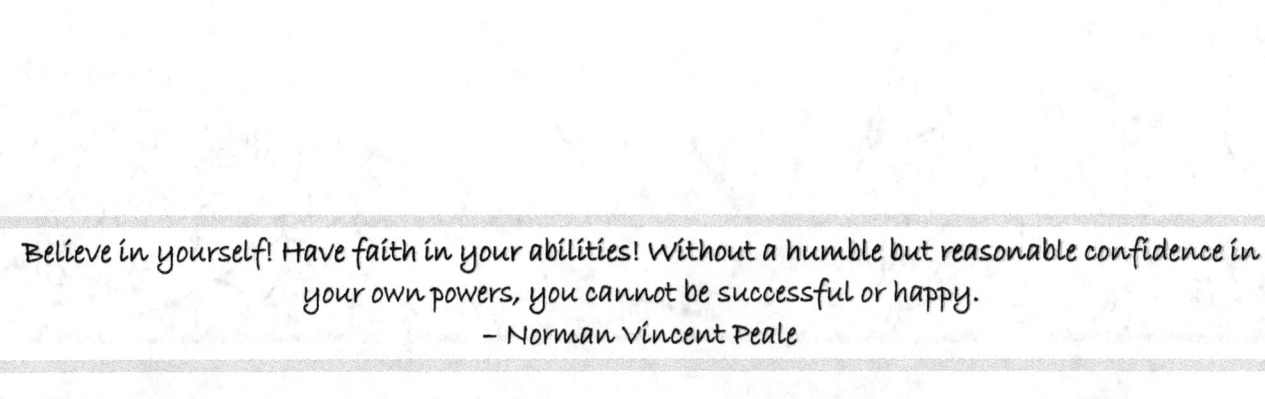

Believe in yourself! Have faith in your abilities! Without a humble but reasonable confidence in your own powers, you cannot be successful or happy.
– Norman Vincent Peale

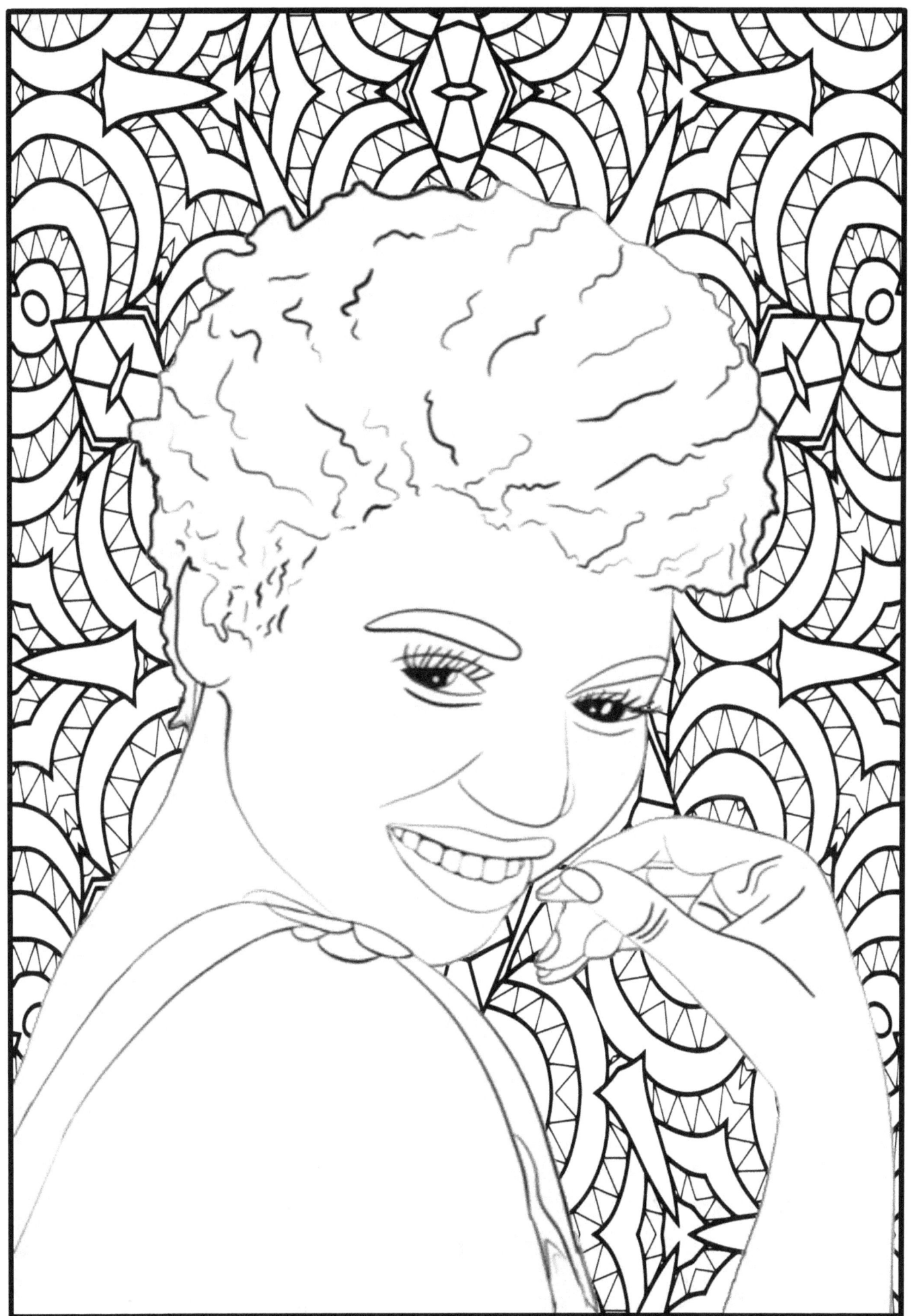

You have to expect things of yourself before you can do them.
– Michael Jordan

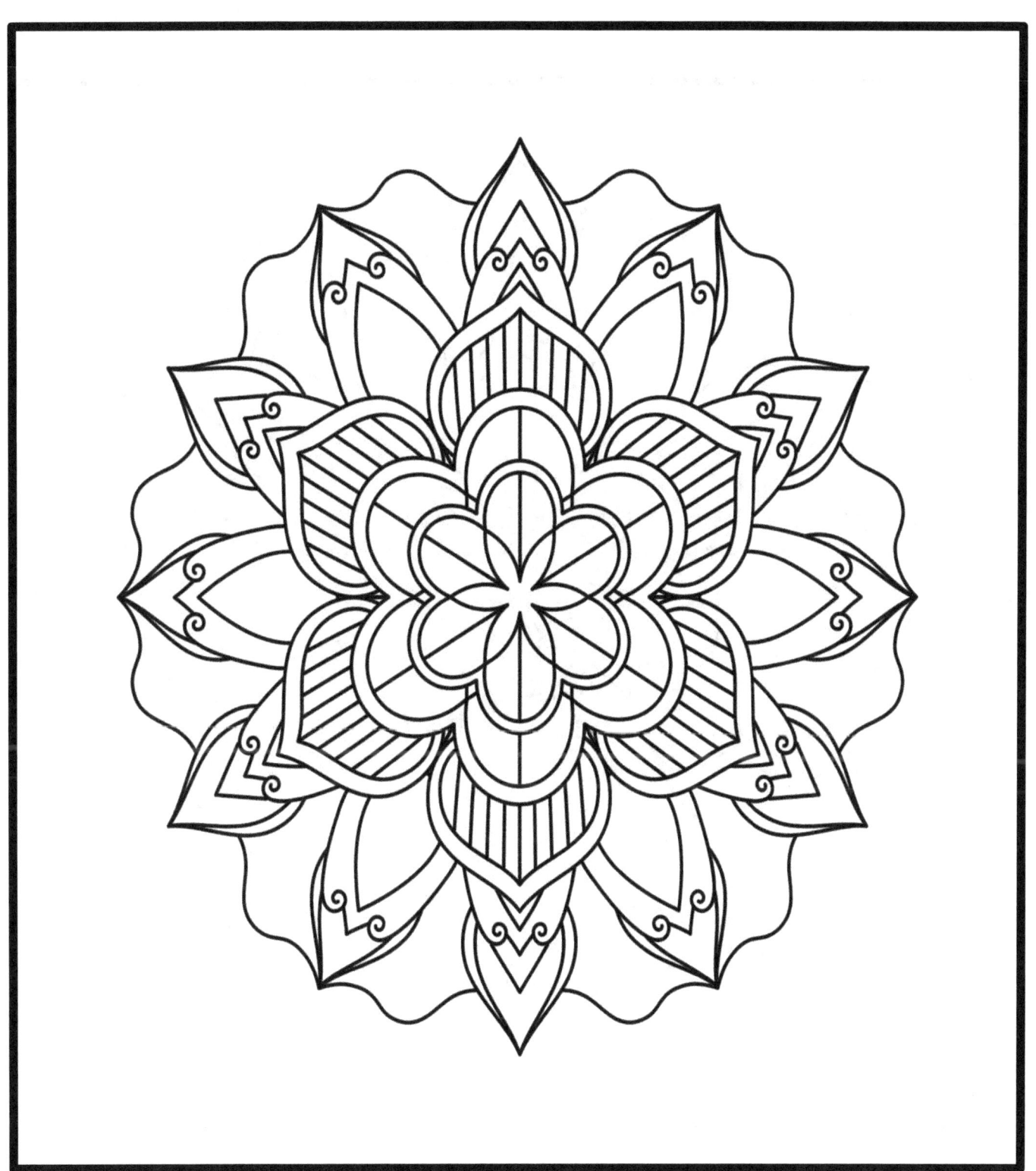

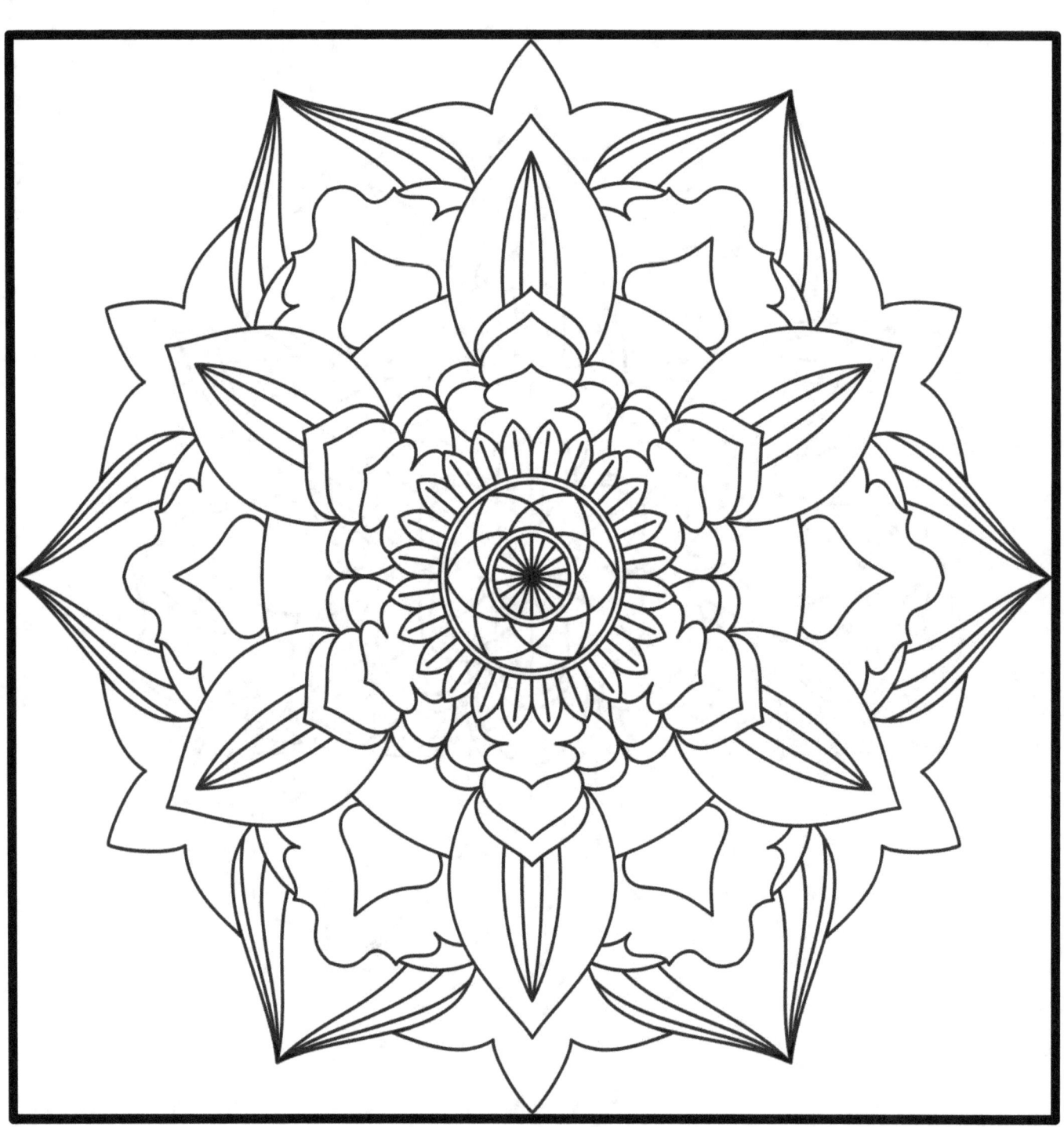

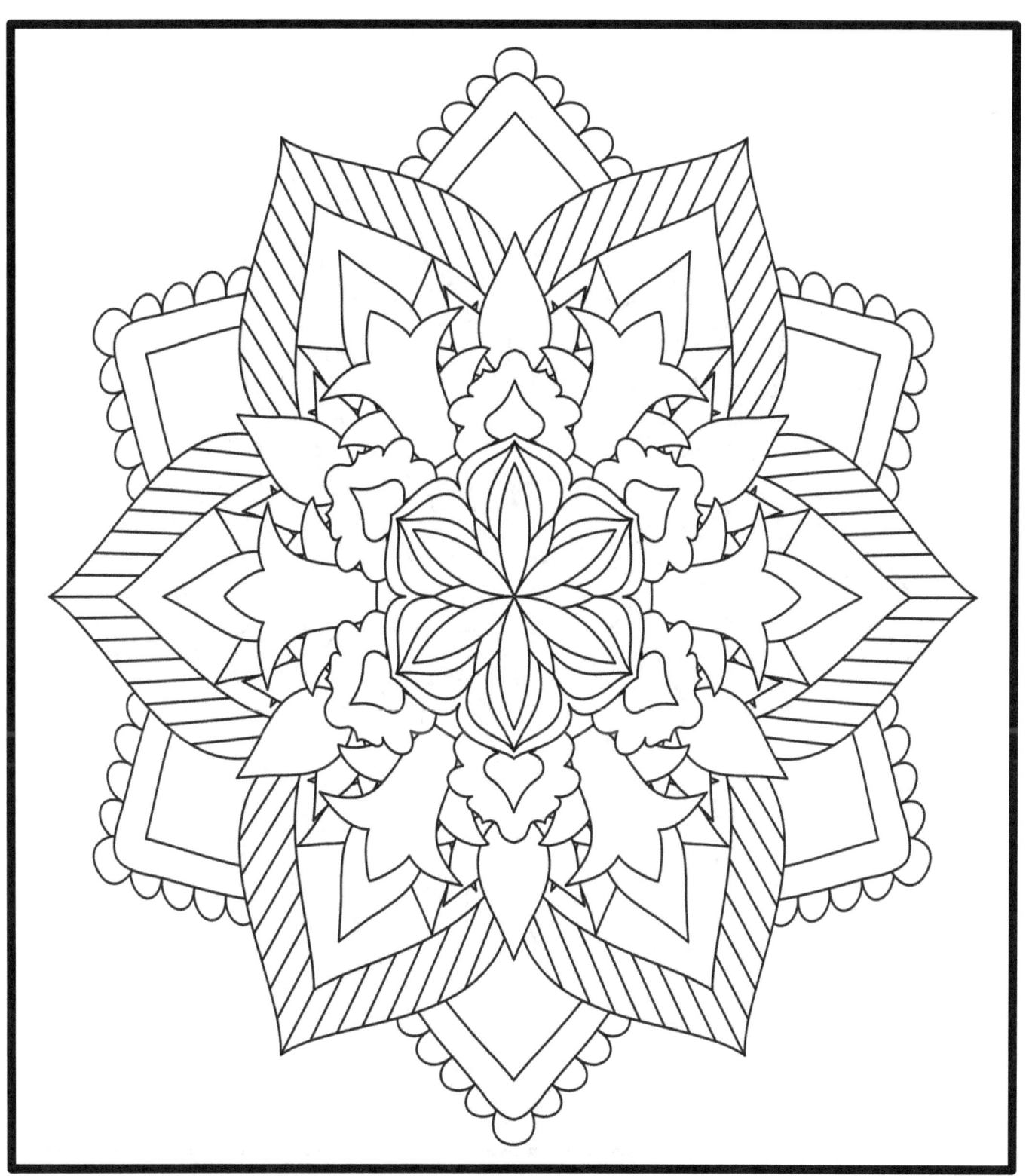

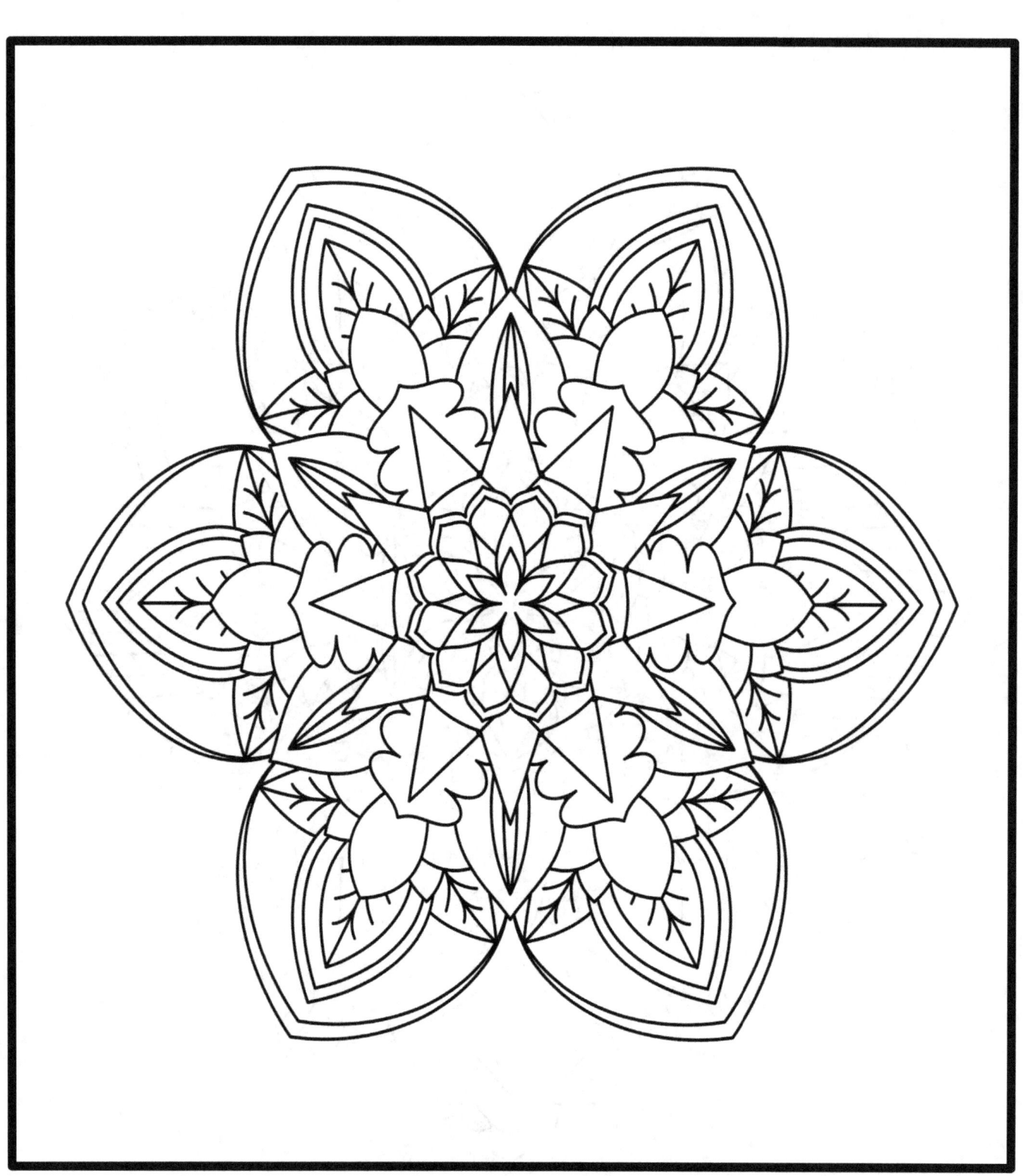

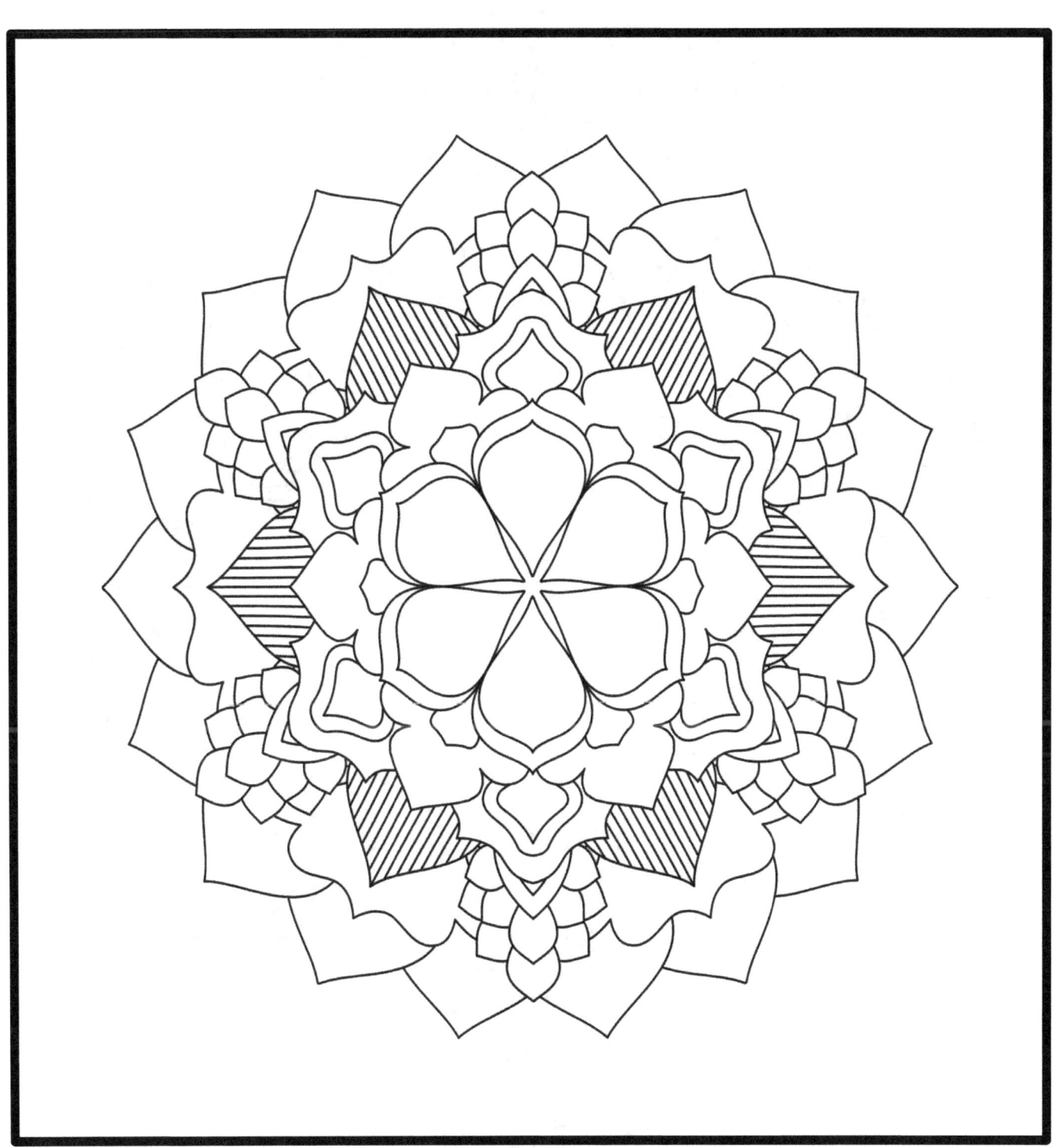

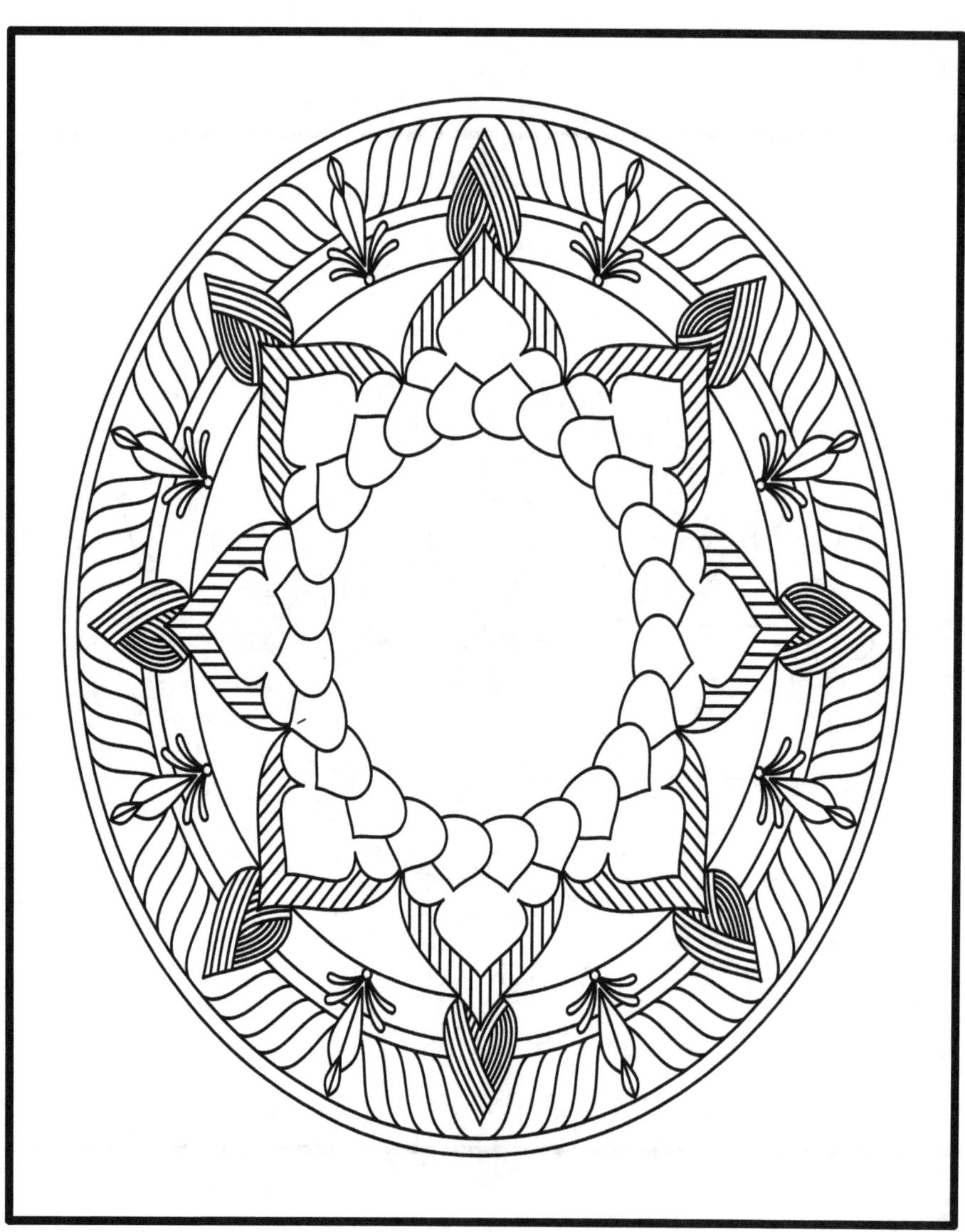